IMAGES
of Aviation

SOUTHERN CALIFORNIA'S
WORLD WAR II AIRCRAFT

Lockheed's P-38 Lightning was radical in nearly every way—nose gear, twin booms, and unusual central pod. Here, a pilot uses the plane's built-in ladder to climb to the cockpit before a bombing mission over Europe. It is worth noting that along with the Burbank-built Lightning, every airplane in this picture was designed and built in California—Mustangs at North American in Inglewood and the C-47 Skytrain at Douglas in Santa Monica. (National Archives, United States Army Air Forces.)

ON THE COVER: New aircraft slowly move along Vultee Aircraft Corporation's automated production line in Downey, California, in 1943. This image shows men and women putting the finishing touches on the SNV training plane, a Navy version of the Vultee BT-13. Though officially named the Valiant, nearly everyone called the aircraft the "Vultee Vibrator." The company made more than 9,500 of them during World War II. (National Archives, Office of War Information.)

IMAGES
of Aviation

SOUTHERN CALIFORNIA'S WORLD WAR II AIRCRAFT

Cory Graff and Patrick Devine

ARCADIA
PUBLISHING

Published by Arcadia Publishing
Charleston, South Carolina

Printed in the United States of America

Library of Congress Control Number: 2016941638

For all general information, please contact Arcadia Publishing:
Telephone 843-853-2070
Fax 843-853-0044
E-mail sales@arcadiapublishing.com
For customer service and orders:
Toll-Free 1-888-313-2665

Visit us on the Internet at www.arcadiapublishing.com

CONTENTS

ACKNOWLEDGMENTS

The authors would like to thank the following people and institutions for their assistance in creating this volume: P. Janine Kennedy, Calvin Graff, and P.J. Müller; Adrian Hunt and Kathrine Browne from the Flying Heritage Collection; Hill Goodspeed from the National Museum of Naval Aviation; Marvin Bailey of the Santa Maria Museum of Flying; Holly Reed and the staff at the Still Pictures Unit of the National Archives; San Diego Air and Space Museum's Alan Renga, Katrina Pescador, and Debbie Seracini; and Matt Todd, Sara Gottlieb, and everyone at Arcadia Publishing.

Photograph credits and sources are noted in parentheses at the end of each caption:

NA/OoWI	National Archives, Office of War Information
NA/USAAF	National Archives, United States Army Air Forces
NA/USAF	National Archives, United States Air Force
NA/USMC	National Archives, United States Marine Corps
NA/USN	National Archives, United States Navy
NMoNA	National Museum of Naval Aviation
SMMoF	Santa Maria Museum of Flying

INTRODUCTION

Southern California became the aviation capital of the world before World War II. A magical mix of favorable flying weather and an abundance of inexpensive land made the southwest coast of California an ideal locale to create winged machines and take to the warm, sunny skies year-round.

Each new aviator or designer who came to the Golden State, it seemed, was drawn by those who had come before. Los Angeles County was the site of America's first air show, held in the winter of 1910. Flyers from colder regions flocked to Dominguez Field (today in Carson, California) to demonstrate their rickety machines. Among the organizers was aviation pioneer Glenn Curtiss from New York. One of the spectators at the event was a wealthy young timber man from Seattle named William E. Boeing. Other future aviation icons in attendance included Glenn Martin, Lawrence Bell, and Donald Douglas.

Glenn Martin established his first airplane "factory" in an abandoned Methodist church in Santa Ana around 1910. The Loughead brothers (pronounced "lockheed") came from the Bay Area to Santa Barbara in 1916, opening their first aviation shop. Waldo Waterman from San Diego came to Venice, California, to create aircraft in 1919. MIT graduate Donald Douglas moved from the East Coast the following year, and T. Claude Ryan migrated west from Kansas to pursue his dreams of flight in 1922.

Each new arrival added more resources to the burgeoning landscape. Besides the wonderful weather and vast acreage, Southern California was a place where these new aviation companies could find educated engineers and designers to make their ideas into reality. Throop Polytechnic Institute (later Caltech) built its first wind tunnel in 1917. In 1919, the University of California Southern Branch (today UCLA) broadened its student pool to include science and letters majors.

These pioneering companies learned from one another too. Jack Northrop worked for Lockheed and Douglas before striking out on his own in 1929. Donald Douglas's first plane, built with David R. Davis, was eventually purchased by T. Claude Ryan in 1925. Douglas had learned his trade working as the chief designer for Glenn Martin. In turn, "Dutch" Kindelberger, who would lead North American Aviation during World War II, also worked for Martin and then became Douglas's chief designer in the 1920s.

Douglas and the Loughead brothers each failed at their first endeavors before establishing major companies that would affect the outcome of World War II. Donald Douglas, after dissolving his partnership with David R. Davis, established Douglas Aircraft Company in 1921. Allan and Malcolm Loughead where forced to close shop in 1921 but formed the new Lockheed Aircraft Company in Hollywood in 1926.

While Lockheed and Douglas began in Southern California, the other two major World War II–era manufacturers, North American Aviation and Consolidated Aircraft Corporation, moved into the area in 1935. North American came from Maryland, looking for enough elbow room to build a large order of planes for the US Army. The company settled in Inglewood, near the current location of Los Angeles International Airport.

Consolidated arrived from Buffalo, New York, for the weather and the water. A tract of land along San Diego Harbor, adjacent to Lindbergh Field, allowed for a reliable (and warm) climate to develop and test both landplanes and their signature flying boats.

Smaller companies made up the Southern California scene too. Ryan Aeronautical Company was Consolidated's neighbor at Lindbergh Field in San Diego. The airstrip was named after Charles Lindbergh, who had become famous for crossing the Atlantic Ocean flying an aircraft designed and built by T. Claude Ryan's first concern, Ryan Flying Company, also in San Diego.

In the Los Angeles area, Jack Northrop formed Northrop Aircraft Inc. in Hawthorne, California, and worked with Donald Douglas to establish the Northrop Corporation, a division of Douglas Aircraft located in El Segundo. Caltech grad Gerard "Jerry" Freebairn Vultee worked for Lockheed, then Douglas, and directly with Jack Northrop before setting out on his own. After many iterations and partnerships, the Vultee Aircraft Division of the Aviation Manufacturing Corporation was formed in 1937 in Downey, California.

Millionaire and movie mogul Howard Hughes Jr. established Hughes Aircraft Company in Los Angeles in 1932, a division of Hughes Tool Company. Hughes's interests were highly focused and usually solo endeavors. After the development of his speedy H-1 racer in 1935, the company's workforce shrank to just four employees. At the height of World War II, however, Hughes Aircraft had a labor force of more than 1,800 men and women building components for military aircraft and developing a pair of flying machines of its own.

Before World War II, California was transformed. The state's population grew by 66 percent in the 1920s, adding 2.5 million new residents. Los Angeles went from the 10th largest city in the United States to number five. It was the highest growth rate since the California Gold Rush. As the Great Depression took hold, 1.5 million more left their homes in the prairie states and the American South to seek a new beginning out West.

New arrivals sought work wherever they could get it, and the US government was there to oblige. The Depression period saw a boom in water projects, new school construction, government facilities, improved airports, and expanded electrical grids for Southern California. Some of the state's most iconic pieces of architecture were built in the 1930s, in part by these migrants from dust-swept regions of America. These included the Golden Gate Bridge, Griffith Observatory, the Bay Bridge, and the expansion of the LA Memorial Coliseum for the 1932 Olympics. And though outside the state, the creation of the Boulder Dam (today called Hoover Dam) was also critical to the needs of Southern California's growth.

War came early for California's airplane companies. Even before the Japanese attack on Pearl Harbor, American aviation factories were flooded with orders. France and Britain wanted warplanes in unprecedented numbers for the fighting in Europe. When France fell to the Nazis in 1940, Britain took over many of the orders for planes already under construction. Simultaneously, the nervous American military attempted to bolster its own air forces for possible, then seemingly inevitable, combat operations.

For foreign orders, Consolidated in San Diego hastily built Liberator bombers and Catalina flying boats. Lockheed made twin-engine patrol planes. And Northrop and Vultee constructed a somewhat outmoded conglomeration of fighters, dive bombers, and attack planes for the cause. Douglas was so overloaded with demand for versions of its twin-engine A-20 attack bomber that it allowed Seattle-based Boeing Airplane Company to make copies of the venerable combat machine under license.

Perhaps the greatest winner in the foreign markets was North American Aviation. In order to quickly teach thousands of military pilots how to fly in Canada, France, Britain, and the United States, North American worked to construct hundreds of training aircraft. And though it had never designed anything like it, North American created a fighter for the British that would change the face of the war. The NA-73, conceived as an improved version of the Curtiss P-40 fighter, would become the famous P-51 Mustang.

The need for manpower and floor space skyrocketed in these tenuous years before America's entry into the war. California factories grew by leaps and bounds. North American's Inglewood facility expanded from 90,000 square feet in 1935, to 160,000 in 1936, to 418,000 in 1939, and to 654,000 in 1940.

The big factories only put the final product fully together. Lockheed's two big plants in Burbank, for example, were supported by a multitude of "feeder" factories—two facilities in Bakersfield, two in Fresno, a pair in East Los Angeles, as well as two more in Santa Barbara, one in Taft, one in Pomona, and a service depot in Van Nuys.

Southern California was quickly becoming crowded. In order to fulfill huge orders, aircraft companies had to fight one another for every press, lathe, and drop hammer west of the Mississippi River. The same went for raw materials—steel I-beams for factory buildings and tubing, sheet aluminum, and electrical wire for new aircraft. Competition for labor meant that company representatives would wander train stations and bus depots looking for able-bodied new arrivals they could draft into service before anyone else even knew they were in town.

The rapidly growing California companies began to look outside the state for satellite facilities in America's heartland. Here, the companies could take advantage of new pools of workers and assure a nonstop flow of airplanes should Japan attack West Coast facilities. North American chose Dallas and Kansas City. Consolidated set up shop in Fort Worth. Vultee choose Nashville. Douglas planes took to the skies from Tulsa and later Chicago.

Factories vulnerable to air attack slipped into the background with the use of camouflage. Netting covered the Ryan and Consolidated factories in San Diego, making their distinctive saw-toothed rooflines blend into the surrounding cityscape. Lockheed in Burbank and Douglas at Long Beach used the magic of Hollywood set designers to make their expansive buildings disappear under a tangle of camouflage netting, chicken wire trees, and artificial houses. From the air, the facilities looked like the surrounding neighborhoods, complete with streets and houses painted onto the tarmac of flat runways and ramp areas.

When the United States went to war in 1941, California aircraft factories were practically set free to produce as many aircraft as possible for the military. While there were still set orders from the government, the numbers of aircraft desired were staggering. Each plane was required almost immediately for combat. As an example, before the Japanese attack on Pearl Harbor, the US Army had 526 fighting aircraft in critical areas of the Pacific. After a few hours of combat, there were only 176 airplanes left.

Declaration of war brought Southern California to a whole new level of madness. On February 23, 1942, a Japanese submarine shelled an oil storage facility in Santa Barbara. The next night, nervous gunners in the Los Angeles area waged a one-hour gun battle with unknown objects in the skies over the city. Known today as the Battle of Los Angeles, the only casualties of the "raid" were the indirect result of the antiaircraft fire, not enemy action.

In this new climate of war, California aircraft companies cooperated, forming the West Coast Aircraft War Production Council (which included the California plane makers and Seattle-based Boeing Airplane Company). Rivals became allies, sharing research, raw materials, and sometimes even employees. When Consolidated and Vultee needed aluminum, Lockheed provided 380,000 feet of Alclad sheet. North American gifted masses of two-inch chrome tubing to Lockheed so it could release badly needed P-38 fighters to the Army. North American learned how to build hearty dive brakes from Vultee designers.

When Northrop's hydraulic press ground to a halt, North American stamped out Northrop P-61 Black Widow parts. By the time Douglas's press gave in, Northrop was again up and running and took on the job. Consolidated's hydropress went next, allowing Douglas to return the favor, stamping truckload after truckload of parts bound for San Diego aircraft.

In wartime, another major blow to airplane producers was the draft. Military services needed men age 18 to 45 in increasingly large numbers—more than 923,000 in 1941, over 3 million in 1942, and more than 3.3 million in 1943. It got to the point where factory officials asked the government to choose: they could have men or they could have planes, but not both. Before the war, Douglas had 77 percent of its workforce that could be drafted. Almost all the rest of the employee base was males out of the age range, designers and engineers critical to the creation of weapons of war, or men physically unfit for service. Women, usually in clerical jobs, made up one percent of the prewar staff.

By 1943, roughly 65 percent of America's aviation workforce was women. With sons, brothers, and husbands off to war, "Rosie the Riveter" came to the factories in huge numbers, running giant drill presses, installing electrical harnesses, cutting metal, and bucking the thousands of rivets that went into each aircraft. As pilots took their new combat planes into battle in Europe and the Pacific, it is no exaggeration to state that their aircraft were built, mostly, by thousands of women back home.

Aircraft companies turned to the African American, Hispanic, and Native American communities for help in large numbers for the first time. Minorities were not commonly treated as equals, and many of them had mixed feelings about helping a nation fight for freedom that was unwilling to grant those same freedoms on the home front.

Always strapped for new workers, California aircraft companies did nearly anything to entice new recruits. They took soldiers who were on leave or men awaiting assignment. They worked deals with schools and technical colleges to grab students for half the day and on Saturdays too. Handicapped persons were given jobs suited to their needs: deaf workers operated uninhibited in the noisiest areas of the factory, blind employees assembled complicated aircraft parts by feel, and companies brought house-bound volunteers tasks they could do from their living room.

North American swept lost hardware off its factory floors by the bucketful. At convalescent homes, residents sorted these castoffs and boxed them so that they could be used again. In this way, the company estimated that citizens saved enough nuts, bolts, and washers to equal the weight of two more B-25 medium bombers.

Company reps cruised bars and pool halls looking for idle hands. They even walked skid rows searching for people to clean up and put to work. Southern California, at least, had a large pool of prospective people to choose from. By 1943, the population of the Los Angeles area was larger than some 37 American states. By the end of that year, San Diego's population had reached half a million.

In order to keep lines of new aircraft flowing smoothly, aircraft companies went out of their way to help workers in any way they could. Company reps would fight parking tickets on a worker's behalf, bring doctors to the factory, pick people up from home, or repair a broken-down car. There was daycare and preschool at factories, as well as branches of the ration board, allowing workers to get back to the planes as quickly as possible instead of waiting in lines. Fifty cents would buy an aircraft builder all the food he or she could eat. Douglas had 37 cafeterias and 13 mobile canteens to keep workers happy, full, and on the job.

There were less subtle motivating factors too. Most factories contained banners and posters designed to boost workers' morale: "Win with Wings" (Douglas), "Navy Pilots are Waiting for These Planes" (Ryan), and "Nothing Short of Right is Right" (Consolidated).

All of the struggles to keep the California assembly lines up and moving paid off for the military and for America. No part of the country or the world built more aircraft during World War II. California warplanes were some of the first into service in North Africa, the first to bomb Japan, and they battered Nazi Germany to the breaking point. The machines from these companies blasted Admiral Yamamoto's aircraft from the skies, deployed paratroopers behind enemy lines on D-Day, sunk Japan's aircraft carriers at Midway, and whittled the once feared German Luftwaffe down to nothing.

Manufacturers in Los Angeles and San Diego turned out 81,596 planes from January 1940 to August 1945. The number was 27 percent of America's total. Including Southern California–designed fighting aircraft built elsewhere in the United States, the count becomes 125,414. That number is an astounding 41 percent of all US military aircraft produced during World War II.

One

CONSOLIDATED VULTEE
AIRCRAFT CORPORATION

The windswept waves of Lake Erie and the Niagara River were no place to develop a new flying boat. When Consolidated's founder Reuben Fleet decided to abandon Buffalo, New York, and move to Southern California, both Los Angeles and San Diego vied for his business. San Diego won out. Fleet had trained there to become an Army pilot in 1917.

In 1935, Consolidated moved, with 157 railway freight cars full of equipment and supplies. Around 400 employees followed, making the trip to sunny California and a new 247,000-square-foot factory at Lindbergh Field in San Diego.

Consolidated's family of successful flying boats led to the development of a workhorse for the Navy's wartime aircraft fleet. More than 3,200 Catalina patrol aircraft cruised the far corners of the globe during World War II, looking for enemy activity. Additional examples served with the US Army and Royal Air Force, operating as antisubmarine, cargo, and search and rescue aircraft.

However, Consolidated's biggest contribution to the war effort came in the form of a large, land-based bomber. The modern B-24 Liberator became a critical key to America's war effort. Consolidated's expanded Liberator lines in San Diego and Fort Worth, Texas, were never enough to keep up with the Army's demand. Additional factories near Dallas, Texas (run by North American), Tulsa, Oklahoma (Douglas), and Willow Run, Michigan (Ford), churned out examples of the vital aircraft at a breakneck pace. In 1944, Willow Run built more than one B-24 *per hour*! Over 18,400 Liberators were built, becoming America's most-produced military aircraft of all time.

At the height of the war, in 1943, Consolidated merged with Downey, California–based Vultee Aircraft Corporation, becoming Consolidated Vultee Aircraft Corporation. Some 7,700 Los Angeles area employees, along with 6,500 of their counterparts in Nashville, Tennessee, worked to deliver a handful of Vultee orders, including Vengeance attack bombers and BT-13 training aircraft. As well, former Vultee workers created components for warplanes being assembled by Consolidated and Lockheed.

At its peak, Consolidated Vultee Aircraft Corporation employed over 99,300 men and women. Consolidated factories built 30,930 military aircraft from January 1940 to August 1945, some 10.3 percent of America's entire air arsenal.

Consolidated needed mild weather and ocean access to perfect its growing line of flying boats. In this image, a pair of PBY Catalinas (foreground), the P4Y Corregidor prototype (left), a Model 24 (center), and a big four-engine PB2Y Coranado share the ramp in front of the then modest-sized Consolidated plant in San Diego in late 1939. (NA/OoWI.)

The first PBY Catalina was completed in 1935 while Consolidated was still based in New York. With the Niagara River frozen over, the plane had to be transported by rail to Naval Air Station Anacostia for testing. This image shows some of the first California-built planes taking shape in August 1936. These first PBY-1 aircraft were delivered to the Navy in October. (NA/USN.)

PBYs were part of America's fighting force from the opening days of the war. This famous image shows the destruction of aircraft, "lined up like ducks in a row," at Ford Island Naval Air Station during the attack on Pearl Harbor, December 7, 1941. Awestruck sailors stand at the wing of a smashed and charred Catalina while another, holed by gunfire, is nearly enveloped by a raging fire. Only three of the 81 PBYs at Ford Island and Kaneohe survived the day unscathed. (NA/USN.)

The Catalina's unique design made it half airplane and half boat. The tough fuselage/hull was joined to a long, wide wing, which positioned its pair of R-1830 engines well above the waterline. Wingtip floats tilted down to provide stability for takeoff and landing. This PBY-5A patrolled convoy routes over the Atlantic late in the war. (NA/USN.)

A spray of icy mud envelops an Alaska-based Catalina loaded with depth charges as it comes in for a landing at an airfield in the Aleutian Islands in March 1943. Far from the tropical islands and palm trees of the South Pacific, Consolidated built PBY patrol planes to operate from anywhere at nearly any time—land, sea, air, and even from snow. (NA/USN.)

Getting a Catalina in and out of the water was not always an easy task, particularly when that water is so cold it is almost solid. Here, a beaching crew uncomfortably retrieves a US Coast Guard PBY-5A in their waterproof cold weather suits at Air Station Kodiak, Alaska, in the winter of 1943. By the end of the war, the Coast Guard operated some 120 PBYs. (NA/USN.)

A pair of "Black Cat" PBY-5As prepare to take off from their base in New Georgia in February 1944. They are assigned to the famous VP-12 squadron—the first designated specifically for night attack missions. With the help of radar and radio altimeters, these aircraft could operate in total darkness, often approaching enemy ships and shore installations just a few feet above the waves to release their torpedoes or bombs. In order to stay unseen, the Catalinas were almost fully covered with matte black paint. (NA/USN.)

Now safely in the fuselage of a PBY, the crew of a downed North American B-25 bomber mugs for the camera after their close call in April 1944. Their aircraft was hit and forced to crash land in the water near the Japanese-held township of Rabaul. A Catalina crew on a Dumbo mission (air-sea rescue) got to the downed crew before the Japanese could, scooping the men from under the nose of the enemy. (NA/USN.)

Patrol flights were long hours of boredom and endless droning over an empty sea followed by seconds of action and terror. Here, a flyer in the waist position of a VPB-63 Catalina aims his heavy .50-caliber machine gun at some ominous object spotted off the coast of North Africa in 1945. (NA/USN.)

Ground crewmen work to load Aleutian-based Catalinas with two varieties of depth charges before a mission. The patrol bomber could carry up to 4,000 pounds of ordnance, including torpedoes and bombs. In this case, the PBYs are patrolling for submarines, carrying weaponry set to sink to a specified depth before exploding alongside a Japanese intruder. (NA/USN.)

Camouflage netting covering Consolidated's factory and ramp offers a bit of shade during a midday break. In the background stands one of an order of 200 PB2Y-3 Coranado aircraft destined to be delivered to the Navy. As one Consolidated worker wrote, the Catalina had sleek fish-like lines, while the enormous four-engine Coranado looked like a "snooty dowager." (NA/USN.)

A massive wooden mock-up takes shape in the Consolidated factory in 1942. The PB3Y project, shelved in 1938, made a comeback with the opening of hostilities. The big plane was designed to carry 22,000 pounds of bombs. This photograph was taken in October 1942; the project was cancelled less than a month later. Note the tail of one of the prototype B-32 bombers at right. (NA/USN.)

The B-24 got its nickname from a contest held among the workers at Consolidated's San Diego plant. Officials chose the anonymous suggestion of Dorothy Fleet, the wife of the company's founder. She nominated the moniker Liberator for the long-range bomber designed to be superior to Boeing's B-17. The modified prototype (XB-24B) is pictured here on a test flight in August 1941. (NA/USAAF.)

The Liberator became the most produced American aircraft of World War II. Factories in Texas, Kansas, Oklahoma, and Michigan churned out the aircraft along with the San Diego plant, seen here. The B-24D in the foreground was assigned to a bomb squadron in England and nicknamed "Big Eagle." On October 9, 1942, it was shot down by German fighters near Dunkirk. It was the first B-24 of the 8th Air Force to go missing. Six of the crew were killed, three captured, and one escaped via Spain. (NA/USAAF.)

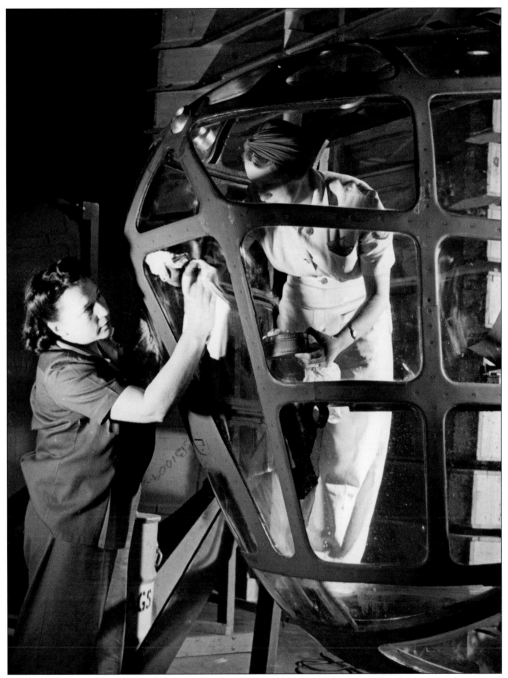

In San Diego, workers Mildred Sherrill (left) and Edna Chamberlain clean the glass noses of Liberator bombers. Most of the aircraft's windows were actually made from clear Plexiglas plastic, which was safer than glass in combat. The only pane that was truly glass was the one that the women are attending to in the center of the nose. The plane's Norden bombsight sighted through this pane, and it was important that there was no distortion. When aerial combat proved that the Liberator was vulnerable to head-on attacks, Consolidated redesigned the nose to carry an Emerson electric turret with twin .50-caliber guns and the flat glass pane in its "chin." (NA/USAAF.)

This image shows the effectiveness of the camouflage netting covering the San Diego plant. Believe it or not, some of the 1.5 million square feet of factory buildings, as well as 1.2 million square feet of outdoor assembly and support space, reside under that blanket of wire, canvas, and faux houses and trees, hiding "the largest integrated covered and uncovered aircraft plant in America," according to a Consolidated press release. This photograph was taken during break time in August 1943. (NA/USAAF.)

A riveting team goes to work on the waist area in the fuselage of a B-24 bomber. Nora McKinnon (left) holds a pneumatic-powered rivet gun while Doris Cook places a bucking bar. The small rivet sits in between them as McKinnon uses her thunderous air hammer to pound the fastener against Cook's steel bar, thus smashing the tail of the rivet and trapping it in place. Both women were waitresses before going to work in the San Diego factory. (NA/USAAF.)

Many parts of the Liberator were built in subassembly factories before being brought together for final assembly in San Diego. Here, a worker at the former Vultee Aircraft plant in Downey, California, spot welds a nearly endless stack of new B-24 tail fins. Vultee and Consolidated merged in March 1943 to create the Consolidated Vultee Aircraft Corporation, often called Convair. This photograph was taken in August of the same year. (NA/USAAF.)

One key to building hundreds of massive aircraft every month was "don't let them get too big, too fast." Every bit of work that could be done to sections of the plane was completed before the components were joined together to build the behemoth bombers. Here, tightly-packed B-24 nose sections take shape in an Office of War Information photograph from August 1943. (NA/OoWI.)

A 513th Bomb Squadron B-24D wades through a deep puddle left by sudden rains in the usually sunny Mediterranean. To keep the big machine from becoming hopelessly sunk in the quagmire, crews have placed rows of pierced steel planking, a portable airfield construction matting used across the world by US aviation units. (NA/USAAF.)

Perhaps the most famous Liberator was a B-24D built at Consolidated in San Diego. The crew of the *Lady Be Good* became hopelessly lost after a bombing mission to Naples on April 4, 1943. Overflying their base in Libya, the plane ran out of fuel at night over the Calanshio Sand Sea of the Libyan Desert. The bomber was discovered in 1958 by an oil exploration team. None of the crewmen who parachuted into the unforgiving landscape were able to walk to safety. (NA/USAF.)

In one of the costliest missions of the war, B-24s of the 15th Air Force attacked nine oil refineries in Romania at low level on August 1, 1943. Some 53 Liberators and 660 flyers were lost in the failed raid. Here, Liberators of the 98th Bomb Group approach their target, code named White IV, the Astra Romana and Unirea Orion refineries near Ploesti. (NA/USAAF.)

Between missions, crews of the 455th Bomb Group brought America's pastime to San Giovanni, Italy. The Ford-built B-24H in the background was named *Snuffy Smith and the Yardbirds*. On May 18, 1943, less than two months after this photograph was taken, the plane was stricken with engine trouble on a mission to Romania and was forced to land at an enemy-held airfield. The entire crew was captured by the Germans. (NA/USAAF.)

Consolidated's B-24 Liberator was superior to the Boeing-created B-17 in many ways. The San Diego–designed heavy bomber was faster, could fly higher, and could carry more bombs. However, the B-24 was never as tough as the B-17 Flying Fortress. Shocking images show Liberators breaking apart in midair after being hit by antiaircraft fire. The plane's thin, efficient, Davis high-lift airfoil wing was its weak point. Above, a Douglas-Tulsa–built B-24H of the 465th Bomb Group trails fire after being hit over Germany in November 1944. Five of the 11 crewmen aboard survived. Below, a Ford-built B-24L, nicknamed "Black Nan," turns over during a bombing mission over Lugo, Italy, in April 1945. A single flyer, thrown from the wreck of the 464th Bomb Group aircraft, survived the crash. (Both, NA/USAAF.)

A pair of gooney birds at Midway Island seem unimpressed as a Liberator of the 11th Bomb Group comes in for a landing in 1943. Four more B-24s can be seen lining up behind the first. The planes were most likely involved in attacks on Japanese-held Wake Island, more than 1,000 miles to the southwest. (NA/USAAF.)

This Consolidated B-24 Liberator was no longer making bombing flights into enemy territory but helping the war effort just the same. Assembly ships were war-weary machines a bit too undependable for combat. Flying units painted the planes in ridiculously bright and distinctive colors and patterns, using them to collect and assemble massive formations of warplanes headed for Germany. (NA/USAAF.)

Lydia Martinez, 19 years old, runs Consolidated's huge hydraulic press at the San Diego plant. Though she is only five-foot-two and 105 pounds, she wields 4,500 tons of pressure to form duralumin aircraft parts for bombers. In Southern California, this type of machine was particularly invaluable to wartime aircraft-building companies. When one of the machines went down, other companies would pitch in, working their hydropress overtime to keep America making as many airplanes as possible. The Williams-White Company, established in 1854, still makes industrial machinery today. (NA/OoWI.)

At an airfield in Italy, a pint-sized pooch seems not the least bit intimidated by the horrid beast looming over him. The flyers called their furry mascot Frank. The plane was named *Howling Wolf* and was part of the 741st Bomb Squadron. The B-24H was lost in a midair collision with another Liberator, *Arkansaw Joe*, over Porto San Stefano, Italy, on April 28, 1944. (NA/USAAF.)

The mud-sprayed belly of *Calamity Jane* of the 725th Bomb Squadron gives some idea of the terrible conditions at the plane's home base in Italy. The plane was nearly wrecked in a forced landing there in September 1944. After repair, the plane was hit by flak over Austria during a strike on an oil refinery on February 7, 1945. The plane and crew failed to return to base. (NA/USAAF.)

If a flyer was going to complain about the Liberator, it was that the aircraft was never as tough as its counterpart, the Boeing B-17. Though fast, high-flying, and able to carry large bomb loads, the B-24 was a delicate machine. Sickening scenes like this haunted B-24 crews. This plane came to grief during a takeoff run at San Giovanni, Italy, on April 12, 1945. The nose gear in the heavily loaded bomber collapsed, horribly crushing the front of the plane as it tipped upward. Six flyers were killed in the crash. (NA/USAAF.)

This underside shot of *Kentucky Belle*, a San Diego–built B-24J of the 706th Bomb Squadron, gives a good view of a pair of the Liberator's aerodynamic features. The corrugated bomb bay doors acted like the cover of a rolltop desk, causing little drag when open. As well, the B-24's retractable Sperry ball turret can be seen aft of the doors. This piece of defensive equipment was only deployed when needed. This photograph was taken over Bottrop, Germany, on November 11, 1944. (NA/USAAF.)

V Grand was the 5,000th B-24 built in San Diego. Autographed by special guests and thousands of employees at Consolidated, the B-24J went to war in the Mediterranean with the 780th Bomb Squadron. After combat, the plane returned to the United States and was stored in Arizona. Sadly, like so many other Liberators, this unique machine was chopped up for scrap in 1946. (NA/USAAF.)

Not all of San Diego's four-engine bombers went to war with the US Army. Some 977 Liberators were assigned to US Navy units, designated PB4Y-1s. This model, equivalent to an Army B-24J, flew with a bow-mounted ERCO ball turret for self-protection or to engage any enemy vessel encountered at sea. Liberator patrol aircraft, in service with the United States and Britain, were credited with sinking roughly 75 German U-boats during their air routes over thousands of miles of open ocean. (NMoNA.)

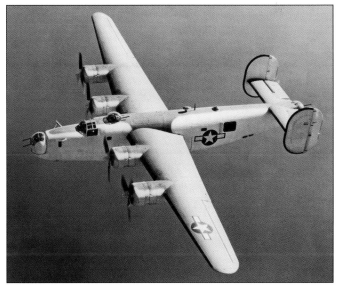

Consolidated designed the longer, lighter Sea Liberator to operate at low altitudes for up to 16 hours. The plane was most recognizable by its tall single tail fin and rudder. Officially dubbed Privateer by the Navy, 739 PB4Y-2 aircraft were made before October 1945. The planes were used exclusively in the Pacific during World War II and continued to serve with the US Navy through the Korean War. (NMoNA.)

One of the most hair-raising parts of any Privateer mission was the takeoff run. Loaded down with bombs, ammunition, and gas, the big patrol planes sometimes struggled to climb into the hot, humid skies from their small island bases. On Marcus Island, engineers did their best and built a runway that extended from one end of the island to the other in order to help the big bombers get every available inch to struggle into the air. This PB4Y-2 ran out of room during a takeoff in 1945 and ended up cracked in half on the sand just a few feet from the Pacific surf. (NMoNA.)

The Liberator airframe was perfect not only for carrying bombs, but also for moving people and cargo. A number of transport versions of the B-24 were built for the military during World War II. This aircraft, designated the RY-3 Liberator Express, was based on the Privateer. The plane could carry 28 passengers or 25,641 pounds of material. (NMoNA.)

War cannot last forever. Consolidated worked with the Navy to build a transport for 48 personnel that used Liberator systems, wings, and engines combined with an expansive new fuselage. The Liberator Liner, seen in San Diego in June 1944, could fly civilians as easily as it could sailors. Consolidated was looking to interest the airlines in the plane once the fighting ceased. (NA/USAAF.)

Consolidated's gargantuan B-32 Dominator had characteristics of the B-24, including a Davis airfoil wing and (originally) big twin tails. The plane was developed in parallel with Boeing's B-29 Superfortress to fill the US Army's "very heavy bomber" role. The project was plagued with technical difficulties, and the original plane crashed at Lindbergh Field in San Diego on May 10, 1943, after just 30 flights. This photograph from April 1944 shows the third aircraft, as well as the twin-tailed second prototype in the background. (NA/USAAF.)

Despite continuing design challenges, the US Army ordered over 1,700 B-32s, the vast majority of which were never built. Though the prototype planes were created in San Diego, production Dominators came from Consolidated's plant in Fort Worth. This is the first Texas aircraft, flown for press photographs. Only a few B-32s made it overseas before the end of World War II. (SMMoF.)

Two

DOUGLAS AIRCRAFT COMPANY INC.

Donald Douglas established his second aircraft company in the back room of a Los Angeles barbershop in 1921. By the late 1930s, Douglas Aircraft was building the famous DC-3 airliner by the hundreds in Santa Monica. By 1939, ninety percent of the world's air commerce flew on DC-3s.

In wartime, existing Douglas DC-3s were commandeered by the government while military versions of the plane emerged from rapidly expanding factories in Santa Monica, Long Beach, and near Oklahoma City. They flew cargo over the Himalayas, crossed the vast reaches of the Pacific Ocean, and deployed paratroopers on D-Day.

Alongside the transports, Douglas built attack planes. After 1941, workers constructed venerable versions of the A-20 Havoc at Santa Monica's maze-like mechanized assembly line. Havocs flew in combat with many Allied nations.

Long Beach and Tulsa, Oklahoma, built the A-20's successor, the A-26 Invader. The bigger, heavier, faster aircraft saw combat in mid-1944. Amazingly, Invaders continued to fly with the US military through the Korean War and Vietnam.

Before America entered World War II, Douglas looked to Boeing to help it build a version of the A-20 attack bomber (designated DB-7) for France and then Great Britain. Later, Boeing turned to Douglas (and Lockheed-Vega) to help keep up with the demand for B-17 Flying Fortress bombers. At Long Beach, Douglas built exactly 3,000 Flying Fortress aircraft for combat.

While Douglas took on the task of creating large-sized workhorses for the Army, the company also produced smaller bombers for the Navy. The Douglas TBD Devastator torpedo plane first flew in 1935 and was outmoded by wartime; however, with no suitable replacement available, the planes soldiered on. At the Battle of Midway, 41 TBDs attacked the enemy's carrier fleet. Only four returned.

While the TBD was a failure, newer Douglas SBD Dauntless dive bombers were the key to victory at Midway. SBDs sunk four Japanese aircraft carriers, turning the tide of the war in the Pacific. The last Dauntless rolled off the assembly line in El Segundo in mid-1944.

At its peak, Douglas employed roughly 160,000 workers. Douglas factories built 30,980 military aircraft from January 1940 to August 1945, some 10.3 percent of America's air arsenal. Douglas, making bigger aircraft, built the most "airframe poundage" of any American aircraft manufacturer—305,573 tons or 15.3 percent of America's total from July 1940 to August 1945.

The Northrop Corporation developed the A-17 attack airplane in the mid-1930s. After Jack Northrop's company was taken over by Douglas in 1937, their El Segundo factory produced improved export versions of the plane, designated the Model 8A. A handful of the planes, ordered by Norway but slated to be transferred to Peru, were commandeered by the US Army and redesignated A-33s. The planes were too outmoded for combat and were used as target tugs, trainers, and utility aircraft throughout the conflict. (NA/USAAF.)

The B-18 Bolo bomber was based on the Douglas DC-2 passenger plane. Almost every B-18 based in the Pacific was ravaged by Japanese attacks in the first days of the war. Those that were left were used as utility and patrol planes. This photograph was taken in happier times as shiny new planes spilled out onto the tarmac in front of the Douglas hangars at Clover Field in Santa Monica in the fall of 1938. (NA/USAAF.)

The concept of very large bombers was at the forefront of the Army's mind in the mid-1930s. Douglas somewhat begrudgingly went along for the ride, creating the biggest airplane in the world. The XB-19 had a gross weight of 81 tons and bristled with defensive guns. Lessons learned designing and building the XB-19 helped make large wartime bombers a reality. In this shot, taken at Santa Monica, flyers ready the aerial giant for flight. (NA/USAAF.)

On June 27, 1941, Maj. Stanley Umstead took the Douglas XB-19 into the skies over Southern California for the first time. Here, the plane, wheels down, is cruising between Venice Pier and Ocean Park Pier. Note the hundreds of oil wells in the Venice area. Umstead's 55-minute test flight took the bomber from Clover Field in Santa Monica to March Field in Riverside. (NA/ USAAF.)

This shot shows a row of C-47 transport aircraft under construction at the Douglas Long Beach plant. The military version of the DC-3 passenger plane was so critical to the war effort that, at times, the men at Douglas worked seven days a week. Women workers, because of California law, got Sunday off. In all, over 10,000 military versions of the DC-3, called Skytrains or Dakotas, were built in Douglas facilities in California and Oklahoma. (NA/USAAF.)

Army Douglas C-47s flew almost everywhere, hauling almost everything, during World War II. Here, an Army Air Forces Air Transport Command Skytrain overflies the Pyramids of Giza near Cairo, Egypt, in 1943. While the actual cargo is unknown, the Army caption states that the plane is loaded with "urgent war supplies and materials, bound for the front." (NA/USAAF.)

In wartime, not only did the War Department build aircraft, it shanghaied whatever it needed from airlines. This camouflaged Army C-47 is actually a Delta Air Lines DC-3; the proof is on the passenger door. Not only has the plane been "drafted" to transport troops and supplies, the Delta crew is now working for Uncle Sam too. In the background is a Delta DC-3 still in civilian livery. This image was captured in May 1942. (NA/USAAF.)

A jaunty-looking crew poses in front of their C-47 they have named *Yard Bird* in New Guinea in March 1943. The name is particularly clever because it could have many meanings. Yard bird is jargon for a chicken in the South. Military men also used the term to colorfully describe an inept soldier or sailor—good for nothing but the most menial tasks. Perhaps the types of jobs left for the men who trudged the South Pacific in a dusty cargo plane. Finally, yard bird meant prisoner. It is quite possible that these flyers, far from home, felt a little like they were doing hard time. (NA/USAAF.)

In front of their trusty C-47 transport, mohawked paratroopers of the 101st Airborne Division apply last-minute war paint before jumping into Normandy in 1944. The men were assigned to secure the causeway exits to Utah Beach, as well as destroy key German-held sites the night before D-Day. Note that the C-47 in the background has black and white "invasion stripes" in order to be easily recognized by friendly fighters and ship-based gunners as they flew over occupied Europe. (NA/USAAF.)

In flight, a group of paratroopers enjoy a last cigarette or joke before leaping into the black skies over enemy-held territory. A Skytrain could hold up to 28 soldiers. Each man had a lanyard connected to the inside of the plane that opened his chute almost immediately after leaving the doorway. Theoretically, this, and a speedy, disciplined exit, ensured that all the men landed in the same area. Note that a censor has blotted out any indication of the GIs' unit and rank and even the label on the man's cigarette package at right. (NA/USAAF.)

A whole book could be filled with nothing but photographs of odd objects being stuffed into the cargo bay of various battered and muddy C-47s throughout the world. This includes donkeys, motorcycles, candy, boats, cows, or barrels of fish oil. Here, a Northwest Airlines crew wrestles a Pratt & Whitney R-1830 Twin Wasp radial engine up a steep ramp. The 14-cylinder engine, bound for Alaska, was probably destined to be installed in another Skytrain stranded in the Aleutians. This photograph was taken in October 1942. (NA/USAAF.)

Men of the 9th Troop Carrier Command awkwardly coax a jeep through the side cargo doors of a Douglas Skytrain somewhere in France. Gen. Dwight D. Eisenhower (later president of the United States) remarked that the C-47 and jeep, along with the 2.5-ton truck and bulldozer, won the war for the Allies in World War II. Interestingly, none of the four were designed for actual combat. (NA/USAAF.)

This Douglas R4D used all of Falalop Island's 3,500-foot runway—and a little more. The men at the Navy base at Ulithi Atoll seem unfazed by the crash; they just want their load supplies and they are willing to wade out into the surf to get it. This accident took place on November 3, 1944. R4D was the Navy's designation for the Army's C-47 Skytrain. If they got to it in time, this plane was likely recovered and repaired. (NA/USAAF.)

The Skytrain's fame not only came from dropping paratroopers on D-Day. The plane was a great tow machine for troop or cargo gliders. Here, a C-47 drags a loaded CG-4A glider into the skies on its single mission, a combat drop over France. The CG-4A weighed nearly 4,000 pounds and could carry slightly more than 4,000 more in soldiers or equipment—a Jeep, a cannon, or 13 troops. (SMMoF.)

Famed writer and flyer Len Morgan related, "The C-47 groaned, it protested, it rattled, it leaked oil, it ran hot, it ran cold, it ran rough, it staggered along on hot days and scared you half to death, its wings flexed and twisted in a horrifying manner, it sank back to earth with a great sigh of relief—but it flew and it flew and it flew." Even on the ground, a Skytrain could be very useful. This "movie night" in the Mediterranean took place sometime in 1944. (NA/USAAF.)

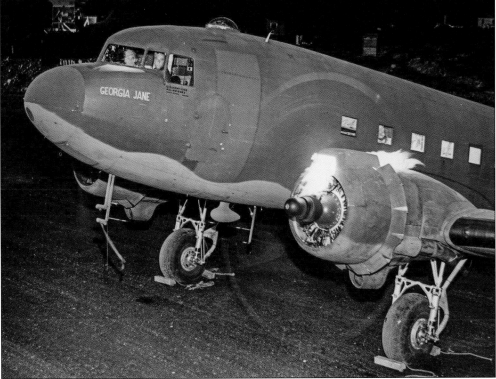

Flames burst from the carburetor inlet of a Douglas C-53 Skytrooper as the plane's Twin Wasp engine coughs to life. The aircraft, an offshoot of the C-47, omitted many of the heavy cargo-carrying features of the Skytrain and focused on simply carrying paratroopers. Only a modest number of 380 Skytroopers were produced at Douglas in Santa Monica because the standard C-47 was so versatile and useful for any task it was assigned. (NA/USAAF.)

The Douglas B-23 Dragon featured the strong wings of a DC-3 with a new, streamlined fuselage. While the plane performed better than the Douglas B-18 bomber, it was beat out during medium bomber trials by another California plane, the North American B-25 Mitchell, as well as Martin's B-26. Only 38 were made at Douglas Long Beach. This is a nearly new B-23 in October 1940. (NA/USAAF.)

Douglas facilities in Santa Monica and one near Chicago built over 1,100 Douglas C-54 Skymaster transport planes from 1942 to 1947. Similar to how the DC-3 airliners spawned the C-47, the Skymaster was a military version of the DC-4 passenger plane. This photograph of a C-54A under construction was taken in mid-1943. The planes served the US military through World War II, the Berlin Airlift, Korea, Vietnam, and beyond. The last plane was retired from US Air Force service in 1975. (NA/USAAF.)

At the factory in Long Beach, Douglas workers put the finishing touches on A-20 Havoc attack bombers headed to combat. In the early years of the war, the versatile plane was not only critical to the American military, but to the British, French, and Russians as well. They saw combat in nearly every theater of war. In this image, a worker has drawn a smiley face in the dust on the Plexiglas canopy of the plane in the foreground. (NA/OoWI.)

The A-20's tight cockpit was similar to that of a fighter airplane. The control yoke, required for the twin-engine machine, is at center with a trigger button for the right thumb. The beam splitter glass of the reflector gunsight can be seen at center, with a traditional ring and bead sight fitted should the reflector fail. At the pilot's left are levers for mixture, pitch, and throttle settings for the plane's Twin Cyclone engines. Note the plastic Douglas logo in the center of the yoke. (NA/USAAF.)

At the Douglas plant in Long Beach, women workers attend to lines of transparent Plexiglas noses of A-20 Havoc attack bombers. The shot was taken by Office of War Information photographer Alfred Palmer in late 1942. The original caption says in part, "Stars over Berlin and Tokyo will soon replace these factory lights reflected in the noses of these planes." (NA/USAAF.)

The crew of a 9th Air Force A-20G (built in Santa Monica) strolls back for debriefing after a mission over France. The flyer at left is the navigator/bombardier. The crewman in the center, holding the plane's modified M2 flexible .50-caliber machine gun, worked as the gunner in the belly of the Havoc. His weapon held enough ammunition to fire for a total of just 30 seconds (400 rounds). The man on the right is most likely the pilot. (NA/USAAF.)

Douglas A-20s of the 671st Bomb Squadron turn toward home after pounding a target near the French coast. In order to effectively hit smaller targets such as airfields, train yards, and coastal positions, twin-engine attack bombers operated at lower altitudes than the larger heavy bombers. Even though they were faster and more maneuverable, they were often exposed to withering antiaircraft fire. (NA/USAAF.)

The company designation for the Havoc was the DB-7 (Douglas Bomber No. 7). As war engulfed Europe, Douglas recruited Seattle-based Boeing Airplane Company to help build DB-7s urgently needed for the Allied cause. When France and Belgium were overrun by the Nazis, Great Britain took over their orders. This flight line photograph, taken in 1941, shows some of the hundreds of DB-7s bound for the United Kingdom. (NA/USAAF.)

Long Beach–built A-20Bs cruise over a parched landscape more than 6,000 miles away from home. Crewmen of the 84th Bomb Squadron almost immediately had their plane's olive drab paint schemes slathered with desert tan spots so that they blended in over French Morocco and Algeria. This image was captured on a low-level bombing mission in late 1942. (NA/USAAF.)

A Santa Monica–built A-20J takes a direct hit in its open bomb bay over the target and catches fire. The image was captured by a 9th Air Force photographer as Lt. R.E. Stockwell's aircraft begins to slowly turn over and go into a spin. The target for the 671st Bomb Squadron on May 12, 1944, was a "noball" site near Beauvoir, France. Noball was the code name for German V-1 and V-2 rocket assembly areas. Two of the four crewmen aboard this aircraft parachuted from the fiery crash and were subsequently captured by the enemy. (NA/USAAF.)

Crewmen strip critical parts from A-20B *Lady Jean* after a wheels-up landing at Youks-les Bains, Algeria. The 86th Bomb Squadron aircraft came to grief after it was hit by antiaircraft fire during a mission on December 31, 1942. The emergency landing was made extra exciting by the fact that *Lady Jean* had a "hung bomb" on one of its outer wing racks. The bomb held in the rack during the rough landing, and everyone walked away from the crash unharmed. (NA/USAAF.)

The Douglas XA-26 prototype was photographed just a few days before its first flight from the Douglas El Segundo factory on July 10, 1942. The new plane was designed as a faster, more powerful replacement for the A-20. Despite difficulties with the nose gear, the plane went into trial service in the Pacific in mid-1943. Large batches of the new attack plane made it to Europe the following year. (NA/USAAF.)

An A-26B pilot wows the crowds at Douglas Long Beach, dodging the corner of the factory building at rooftop level. Amazingly, this aircraft still survives today. The preserved warbird sits in the courtyard of South Mountain High School in Phoenix, Arizona. South Mountain is a magnet school for aviation and aerospace education. (NA/USAAF.)

Perhaps the most notable thing about the Douglas A-26 was its long combat career. After the battles of World War II were over, examples of the plane went on to fly in Korea, Vietnam, and beyond. Long Beach–built *Myakinazz* of the 730th Bomb Squadron was used to hunt North Korean trains and trucks. This photograph of the plane's air and ground crew was taken at Pusan East Airfield in February 1951. The aircraft is loaded down with eight .50-caliber guns, five-inch rockets, and bombs. As well, the aircraft carries a pair of 75-gallon external fuel tanks to maximize its time over the area of operations. (NA/USAAF.)

The Boeing Airplane Company's B-17 Flying Fortress heavy bomber was so critical to the war effort that two Southern California companies, Douglas and Lockheed, built the plane under license. This photograph shows a long line of B-17F aircraft in final assembly at Douglas Long Beach in June 1943. In the early years of the Cold War, Douglas would again build a Boeing aircraft, the B-47 Stratojet. (NA/USAAF.)

A Douglas factory worker makes final adjustments to the mount for the B-17's fabled Norden bombsight. The analog computer could be linked to the plane's autopilot, allowing for more accurate bomb strikes from high altitude. The nose compartment of the Flying Fortress held two flyers in combat, the bombardier and navigator. The crewmen also manned defensive guns to ward off attacking fighters. (NA/OoWI.)

A Long Beach–built B-17G Flying Fortress lumbers into the target area in southeast Germany. The target for this day, February 5, 1945, was the oil storage facility near Regensburg. The aircraft was assigned to the 774th Bomb Squadron based in Italy. Of the 12,731 B-17s constructed during the war, Douglas Aircraft built exactly 3,000. (NA/USAAF.)

Women workers install fixtures and assemblies in the aft fuselage of a Douglas-built B-17. The windows on either side are the plane's waist gun positions, manned in flight by a pair of gunners. This is a B-17F. Later, improved G-model aircraft had the windows staggered so the two crewmen would not bump into each other while firing at attacking enemy aircraft. (NA/OoWI.)

Large batches of Douglas-built B-17s were further modified for search and rescue work. An SB-17 (S for search and rescue) was often stripped of much of its defensive armament and combat equipment. The plane carried a 25-foot A-1 lifeboat that could be dropped, via parachute, to a downed airman. "Dumbo" SB-17s, assigned to emergency rescue squadrons, saved many fighter pilots and bomber crewmen from the cold English Channel or the vast reaches of the Pacific. (NA/USAAF.)

The ineffectiveness of the Douglas TBD Devastator torpedo bomber in the opening months of World War II had a lot to do with the plane's age. It was the first widely used carrier-based monoplane and the first all-metal naval aircraft. Before the Devastator, the US Navy flew cloth-covered biplanes. This mock-up (which is more cloth and wood than metal) was made by Douglas engineers to show the general layout of the TBD-1 to the Navy's Bureau of Aeronautics. The photograph was taken in April 1934. (NA/USN.)

A prewar scene shows TBD-1s coming together at Douglas in Santa Monica. The plane in the foreground was assigned to VT-2 (Torpedo Squadron 2). The plane was reported to have gotten a torpedo hit on the Japanese light carrier *Shoho* during the Battle of the Coral Sea on May 7, 1942. The plane would be lost the following day when the USS *Lexington* was sunk by Japanese torpedo bombers. (NA/USN.)

A TBD-1 assigned to VT-6 aboard the USS *Enterprise* cruises Wake Island during attacks on the Japanese-held atoll. At the Battle of Midway, more than three months later, VT-6 lost 10 of their 14 Devastators on the morning of June 4 while attacking enemy aircraft carriers. This plane was most likely among them. After Midway, the Navy withdrew the surviving TBDs (about 39 of them) from front-line service. (NMoNA.)

After minor repairs and alterations at Pearl Harbor, the USS *Enterprise* heads back to sea in April 1942. The ship's forward flight deck is stuffed with Douglas SBD Dauntless dive bombers of VS-6 and VB-6 (as well as a few Grumman Wildcat fighters). The SBD (Scout Bomber, Douglas) started life as a Northrop design in 1935. When Douglas took over the Northrop Corporation, it continued work on the design. The Dauntless was well-liked by naval aviators for its ruggedness and great diving characteristics. (NA/USN.)

Douglas-built SBD Dauntless dive bombers won the Battle of Midway, their bombs destroying four Japanese aircraft carriers, three of them in just six minutes of combat. Here, SBD-3 aircraft assigned to VS-8 of the USS *Hornet* approach the mortally wounded Japanese heavy cruiser *Mukuma* with 1,000-pound bombs on June 6, 1942. The ship sank later that day. (NA/USN.)

Major Elmer Glidden Jr. (left), commander of the Marine Corps VMSB-231, oversees the application of bombing mission tallies on the side of his Douglas SBD-6 Dauntless aircraft in the Marshall Islands. Glidden had over 104 combat bombing missions to his credit by the end of the war. Aviators often joked that SBD (Scout Bomber, Douglas) actually stood for "slow, but deadly." (NA/USMC.)

A long row of SBD-5 Dauntless aircraft are finished at the former Northrop plant taken over by Douglas in El Segundo. This photograph was taken in 1943 as the shifts changed. Commonly, the floor was a mass of activity seven days a week. At most hours, day and night, the building was a cacophony of sound. As one worker related, "We were supposed to wear earplugs, and not everybody wanted to do that, but it sure helped a lot. If you couldn't hear anyway, you might as well wear the earplugs." (NA/USN.)

A Douglas SBD gets pulled ashore on what looks like a tropical paradise. Though there was no fighting there, Espiritu Santo in the New Hebrides Islands was a forbidding outpost of heat, humidity, flies, and disease-carrying mosquitos in mid-1942. The island did have a 6,000-foot runway however, which the Navy carved from the jungle in just 20 days. The base quickly grew to be the second-largest US base in the Pacific, behind Oahu. (NA/USN.)

Shot up and low on fuel, this SBD-3 from VB-6 landed on the USS *Yorktown* during the Battle of Midway. Many of the planes from the squadron failed to return from attacks on the Japanese fleet on June 4, 1942. This photograph of the damaged Dauntless inspired a Douglas Aircraft Company advertisement with a painting of a badly blasted SBD returning to a carrier. The tagline was, "Coming in on a Wing . . . and Douglas dependability." (NA/USN.)

The sun set on the career of the Douglas SBD before the war came to a close. The Navy chose to switch to a bigger and faster aircraft designed by Curtiss-Wright. The new aircraft was not popular with many naval aviators and some flyers demanded the return of the dependable and tough Douglas SBDs. The last SBD came off the assembly line at El Segundo in mid-1944, and the plane's last major combat took place at the Battle of the Philippine Sea in June of that same year. (NA/USN.)

Over 60 percent of the workers at Douglas were female. Department 50 at Santa Monica was exceptional in that 100 percent of the staff were women. Here, some of the ladies work on the tail controls of A-20 bombers. Factories mandated that long hair and bangs had to be tied up in a head scarf to keep an unlucky worker from getting stuck in an unforgiving electric drill or singed by a spot welder. (NA/OoWI.)

Over the course of a day, hundreds of nuts, bolts, and rivets skittered across the factory floor and out of reach. Periodically, someone would sweep up, leaving massive piles of metal shavings, trash, and a plethora of unused hardware. Here the women at Douglas work to sort the "wheat from the chaff," putting lost fasteners back into service. This recovery process saved the company (and the American people) thousands of dollars. (NA/OoWI.)

A public relations photographer gathered these four Douglas women laborers in order to illustrate the diversity of the workforce in Southern California. The original World War II–era caption awkwardly introduces, from left to right, "Mexican Josephine Lujan, Chinese Jane Lee, Negro Dorothy Spencer, and Nordic Roberta Norton." Beyond the fact that women were stepping into the workforce in large numbers for the first time, many minority populations were almost completely ignored by aircraft companies until wartime needs forced their hand. (NA/OoWI.)

During the war years, Douglas designers began work on a particularly radical bomber powered by a pair of Allison engines and pusher propellers. The XB-42 could fly far and fast. Despite its excellent performance, the end of hostilities, as well as the emergence of jet aircraft, put an end to this unusual aircraft. This photograph shows the first of two prototypes in May 1944. (NA/USAAF.)

An aircraft that would become a workhorse of American forces in Korea and Vietnam took its first flight during World War II. The Skyraider was designed in El Segundo as a replacement for the Douglas SBD Dauntless dive bomber. For a brief time, the new carrier-based bomber was called the Dauntless II. The plane's first flight took place on March 18, 1945, and though it was too late to enter combat, early testing proved the big attack plane to be worthy of becoming part of the Navy's postwar air fleet. Production continued until 1957. (NMoNA.)

Three

LOCKHEED AIRCRAFT CORPORATION

Before World War II, Lockheed was struggling to find its niche building passenger planes. Improved versions of the twin-engine Electra were barely keeping the company afloat. The breakthrough came in 1938, when the Royal Air Force ordered 200 examples of the Model 14 Super Electra as patrol bombers. The order gave the Burbank-based company stability and allowed expansion.

The Army ordered the plane too, along with versions of the bigger Lockheed Model 18, using them as cargo haulers, bombers, and VIP transports. The Electras were also the jumping-off point for the Navy's PV-1 Ventura and PV-2 Harpoon patrol planes. Some 5,600 "Electra Family" aircraft were built for the military.

Lockheed is perhaps most famous for its iconic fighter, the P-38 Lightning. First flown in 1939, the Lightning was the first fighter to attain speeds over 400 miles per hour. The radical aircraft had a tricycle landing gear, heavily armed center pod, and distinctive twin tail.

P-38 Lightnings served in nearly every theater of war, from North Africa to the Aleutian Islands. America's top all-time ace, Richard Bong, flew a Lightning in the Pacific, tallying 40 victories. The California-built plane holds the distinction of being the only American fighter in production throughout the entire war.

A bomber with a similar production record was Boeing's B-17 Flying Fortress. Vega Aircraft Corporation, Lockheed's subsidiary until 1943, license-built B-17s in Burbank, generating some 2,750 four-engine bombers by war's end.

Lockheed's new passenger plane, developed in cooperation with Howard Hughes's Trans World Airlines, served as a massive cargo aircraft during the war. First flown in 1943, the modern and graceful looking C-69 Constellation hauled troops and equipment before becoming one of the most popular and iconic airliners of the postwar boom.

Lockheed's secret aircraft division, known as the "Skunkworks," got its start in 1943 working on the Army's first operational jet fighter. The Lockheed P-80 Shooting Star first flew in 1944. A handful of the planes were deployed overseas in the last months of the war, but none saw combat in World War II.

Lockheed built 19,078 planes from January 1940 to August 1945, representing 6.3 percent of America's total output. At the height of employment, Lockheed had 93,000 men and women on its staff.

Numerous versions of Lockheed's versatile twin-engine aircraft, derived from the Model 14 and 18, flew with US Army, Navy, and Allied air forces during World War II, such as the Lodestar, Lexington, Ventura, Harpoon, and Hudson. A Navy writer carefully noted that this plane is an Army B-34 Ventura taking off at Guadalcanal in the original caption. The planes were used for patrol, bombing, hauling cargo, training, and attack duties all over the world. (NA/USN.)

Workers at Lockheed's plant in Burbank discuss the fit of the aft door of a new Navy PV-1 Ventura in June 1943. In the foreground, hard noses stand upright as metal skins are prepped for riveting. Early versions of the plane had glass in the nose for a bombardier's station. Most Venturas came from the factory with a solid nose equipped with two or three .50-caliber guns. (NA/USN.)

Even for a long-legged patrol plane like the Ventura, some distances were just too much to handle. In order to get planes quickly into the Pacific, they were often packaged, then loaded onto escort carriers or cargo ships. Braving the cold, a Lockheed official looks on as the planes are craned into place and strapped down for their journey. (NA/OoWI.)

The huge gaggle of California planes in this photograph are a long way from home. Seen in May 1942, Lockheed Hudsons and Venturas join North American B-25 Mitchells, a Boeing B-17, and Consolidated B-24 Liberators, all bound for England. The scene took place at Dorval Airport, just west of Montreal, Canada. Nearly all are Lend-Lease aircraft (military aid to allies) that carry the roundel of the Royal Air Force. (NA/USAAF.)

The crew of a Lockheed Ventura, looking absolutely beaten, forlornly await the salvage trucks after a landing mishap in 1941. The plane was most likely involved in a ground-loop accident that collapsed the starboard main gear. Their once beautiful machine now lies dented and smashed, sprayed with mud and fire retardant foam, at Coast Guard Air Station Elizabeth City in North Carolina. (NMoNA.)

At a base in the Aleutians, crewmen load 500-pound bombs into the belly of a Lockheed PV-1 in June 1943. Early in the war, Japanese forces had occupied the islands of Attu and Kiska—the only US soil that Japan would claim during World War II. As spring broke in 1943, American forces pushed back, reclaiming the territory. The area, known for harsh terrain and unpredictable, brutal weather, was a nightmare for flyers. (NA/USN.)

The first US Marine PV-1 crew in the Pacific is briefed before a patrol from the Russell Islands in September 1943. The unit, VMF(N)-531, often flew at night, attempting to track Japanese aerial intruders and blast them from the inky skies. Their first victory came in November when a Marine Ventura attacked an enemy G4M Betty bomber at 4:30 a.m. near Bougainville Island, sending it into the sea in flames. (NA/USMC.)

Lockheed's P-38 was an amazingly radical departure from traditional fighter design. Twin engines with contra-rotating propellers, bulbous center pod, and long double booms made the Lightning instantly recognizable to friend and foe alike. This is the XP-38A, photographed over the sprawling city of Los Angeles in June 1942. (NA/USAAF.)

As Lockheed's Burbank P-38 plant received a new automated conveyor belt system, workers moved outside to continue the long line of badly needed Lightning fighters for combat. This photograph was taken in June 1943—an ideal time to work in the Southern California sun. When the new factory was ready for airplane assembly, it took nine days to move a new P-38 down the line and out the door. (NA/USAAF.)

A Lockheed P-38 fighter, fresh from the Burbank factory, is loaded into the hull of cargo ship SS *Raymond Van Brogan* in April 1945. The plane was bound to join a fighter squadron deployed to the Pacific. The plane's smooth form is encased in a spray-on anticorrosion covering called Plastiphane. At its destination, ground crew would remove the coating, revealing the new fighter underneath. (NA/OoWI.)

This is a Mk I Lightning, photographed in California before being transferred overseas. Originally, European buyers wanted versions of the plane without superchargers and equipped with two standard right-hand rotating props. Lockheed began to deliver them as specified, but factory workers secretly called the planes "castrated P-38s." Ultimately, most of the order was retained and modified by the US Army to be trainers and experimental test beds. (NA/USAAF.)

In Alaska, the Army did anything it could to keep it fighters flying. Here, crewmen use a dogsled to deliver fuel out to the frozen airfield. The twin-engine P-38 used roughly twice as much fuel as a plane like the Curtiss P-40. Note the heavy tape covering the Lightning's guns to keep out the moisture, frost, and cold. (NA/USAAF.)

Lockheed's P-38 Lightning packed a punch. Most fighter aircraft of the era had guns in the wings, set up to converge at 300 or so yards in front of the plane. The Lightning had four .50-caliber machine guns and a 20-mm cannon (seen at center) tightly packed in its nose, throwing out a concentrated barrage of lead into the skies. As a result, enemy pilots avoided approaching a P-38 head-on. (NA/USAAF.)

The escort becomes the escorted as this Lightning limps toward home with friends. The plane's starboard engine has violently died, leaving a spray of oil all the way back to the tail. The photograph was taken by a crewman in a heavy bomber that was offering protection to the wounded fighter. The B-17G Flying Fortress closest to the camera, assigned to the 96th Bomb Squadron, was built at Douglas Long Beach. It was lost on August 2, 1944. This image was captured over Blechhammer, Germany, on July 7. (NA/USAAF.)

Stunned pilot Lt. Thomas Smith looks over his gravely wounded P-38 after a hard landing in Italy. A German Bf 109 hit the plane head-on, smashing its starboard engine and chopping through the horizontal stabilizer between the Lightning's tail booms. While the Bf 109 tumbled to the ground, the Lockheed machine brought Smith home with only a nasty bump on the head. (NA/USAAF.)

Ground crewmen, acting as dead weight, shoot the breeze as they wait for their buddies to change the nose wheel of a 474th Fighter Group Lightning based in France. It was a welcome break from the nonstop work at a busy 9th Air Force airfield not too far from the front lines. The Lightning's nose landing gear was unique. Most fighters of the era were "tail-draggers," with a small wheel in the back. (NA/USAAF.)

As if being wounded in wartime was not terrifying enough, the US Army Air Forces experimented with exint pods, capable of carrying a wounded man under the wing of a fighter like the P-38. This one is being used by a reconnaissance P-38 (designated F-5) to give a photographer the view of a lifetime through the Plexiglas nose of the pod. (NA/USAAF.)

During the battle for Okinawa in June 1945, Marine Corps Corsairs stick very close to a 28th Photograph Reconnaissance Squadron F-5E (P-38) named *Information Please*. The reason for the heavy escort is clear when it is noted that the plane carries one very brave USMC combat photographer in the pod slung under its belly. It makes for a good photograph, but should the unarmed plane get painted into a corner it is up to the Corsairs to come to the rescue—there would be no way for the photographer to bail out. (NA/USAAF.)

This is as close to a family portrait as one can get in wartime. The pilot is Col. Harold J. Rau, commander of the 20th Fighter Group. The 20th FG was particularly adept at destroying German trains, which earned them the nickname "Loco Busters." Here, Rau poses with his ground crew and his dog, Honey. They stand in front of *Gentle Annie*—named after the popular song. Rau flew four P-38s during his 27 months in combat. He is credited with destroying numerous trains, one enemy plane in the air, and four more on the ground. (NA/USAAF.)

America's all-time top ace claimed all of his aerial victories flying the Lockheed P-38 Lightning. In combat, Richard Bong shot down 40 Japanese aircraft and earned the Medal of Honor. Late in the war he became a test pilot assigned to Lockheed's plant in Burbank. He was killed in the crash of a P-80 jet fighter, which fell near the corner of Oxnard Street and Satsuma Avenue in North Hollywood on August 6, 1945. (NA/USAAF.)

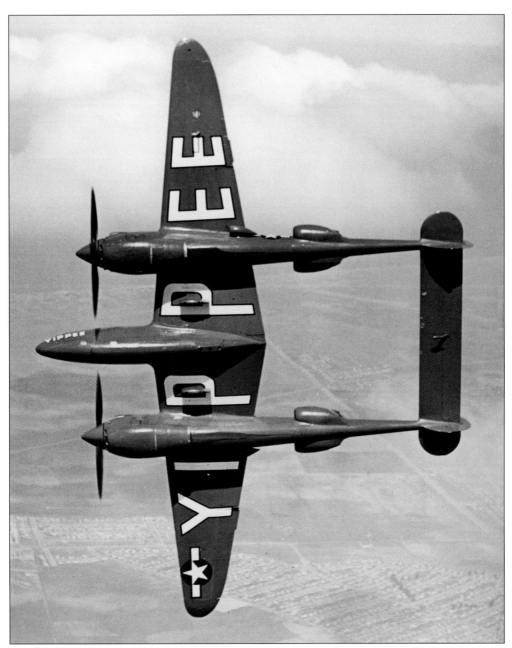

Yippee was a P-38J, the 5,000th Lightning off the production line at Burbank. The plane was briefly painted bright red for promotion and public relations purposes, but soon enough, workers stripped off the distinctive scheme, and it joined a group of fighters headed into combat in the Pacific. The briefly famous P-38 was assigned to the 431st Fighter Squadron and was involved in an aerial accident in early 1945 near the Philippines. It never returned to the United States. (NA/USAAF.)

If looks made an airplane fly, this one would have stayed firmly on the ground. The Lockheed XP-58 Chain Lightning was an offshoot of the P-38 design, made to fly at high altitude for long distances. Troublesome engines, changing design specs, and mechanical complications hindered the program for years. On June 6, 1944, the first and only prototype lifted off on its maiden flight from Burbank to Muroc Field (today Edwards Air Force Base). By the time the Japanese surrendered, the project was dead. (NA/USAAF.)

As a trio of companies worked to build the 10,000th B-17 Flying Fortress, the public relations folks carefully orchestrated a milestone event. Seattle-based Boeing, the designer of the plane, would build 10,000. The 9,999th plane would come from the Douglas plant, and number 10,001 would be a Lockheed-Vega product. Here, all three are posed briefly for newspaper photographs at Long Beach in October 1944. (NA/USAAF.)

Lockheed worked with the Army to develop a "wolf in sheep's clothing," a converted Flying Fortress that carried nothing but guns and ammunition. Lockheed modified a Seattle-built plane and then went on to make 24 of their own. The "gunship" program was only partly successful because when the regular bombers let loose their several thousand pounds of bombs, they suddenly were much lighter and faster than their guardians. This image shows a Lockheed-built YB-40 relegated to stateside gunnery training. (NA/USAAF.)

During wartime, military forces experimented with drone aircraft converted into remote-flying bombs. This Burbank-built Flying Fortress had a brief life after the war as a CQ-17, the mother ship to a group of QB-17 drones. Operating with the 58th Wing, the plane worked from Eniwetok Atoll, about 210 miles from Bikini Atoll. Bikini was the site of atomic bomb tests during Operation Crossroads in 1946. (NA/USAAF.)

Howard Hughes's dream airliner was temporarily derailed by wartime demands. The first Lockheed Constellation passenger planes went to the Army as C-69 cargo aircraft. This is a C-69 temporarily decked out in TWA colors, along with an old workhorse TWA Douglas DC-3. The Army allowed the Lockheed C-69 to complete a record-setting dash across the United States with Howard Hughes and TWA president Jack Frye at the controls on April 17, 1944. They traveled from Burbank to Washington, DC, in six hours and 58 minutes. (NA/USAAF.)

Lockheed's P-80 Shooting Star was America's first operational jet fighter. First flown in 1944, Lockheed worked to rush jet aircraft into service before the war ended. Two YP-80As were sent to England and two more to northern Italy. The planes were flying (only locally) in early 1945. None saw combat. This aircraft was a P-80A, later upgraded to P-80C standards with an improved engine and ejection seat. (NA/USAAF.)

A visitor takes a look at the "working end" of a P-80 during an open house in Washington, DC, on August 1, 1945. The plane's engine was an Allison-built J33-A centrifugal-flow turbojet designed by General Electric. For the old-school "prop jockeys," the sensation of being pushed through the skies without torque or vibrations was strange but exhilarating. (NA/USAAF.)

The true era of the jet arrived in the years after World War II. America's desire to have the most effective technology to challenge the Soviet Union in Europe kept Lockheed building P-80s even after many wartime contracts were cancelled. This photograph shows lines of P-80s ready for service at Fürstenfeldbruck Air Base in Germany in May 1949. They were assigned to the 36th Fighter Wing. (NA/USAAF.)

Four

NORTH AMERICAN AVIATION

North American Aviation (NAA) began life in 1928 as a Maryland-based holding company. It became an operating aviation manufacturer in 1934 and moved to sunny California the following fall. About 75 employees made the trip to Inglewood, California, in order to begin production of a new trainer aircraft for the Army Air Corps.

NAA began work in a 90,000-square-foot factory building on the corner of Imperial Highway and Aviation Boulevard, which is today on the grounds of Los Angeles International Airport. Rent was $600 a year.

Improved versions of its original BT-9 trainer aircraft led to the first of a trio of World War II icons, the more sophisticated AT-6 Texan. As the world moved closer to war, NAA not only built these aircraft to help train US Army and Navy pilots, but also flyers in Britain and France. By 1938, over 3,000 people worked at North American on orders for 399 planes.

In 1939, NAA's medium bomber prototype took to the skies for the first time. It was the biggest and most complex aircraft the company had ever created. The machine, soon to be named the B-25 Mitchell by the Army, would be the second of North American's three famous war machines.

When Germany invaded Poland in 1939, orders increased dramatically. Soon after, North American established factories in Dallas and Kansas City to help keep up with demand. The British, desperate for fighter aircraft, also spurred North American to develop the P-51 Mustang—considered one of the best airplanes of all time.

As America went to war, most Allied pilots finished their training in North American aircraft. B-25 Mitchells fought in nearly every theater of the conflict and became famous when James Harold "Jimmy" Doolittle used 16 of the planes to launch a carrier-borne air strike on Japan in 1942. Squadrons of P-51 Mustangs helped escort heavy bombers over "Fortress Europe" and paved the way for the D-Day landings by sweeping the skies of Luftwaffe aircraft.

At its peak, North American Aviation employed over 91,000 men and women. NAA factories built 41,839 military aircraft from January 1940 to August 1945, more than 13.9 percent of America's entire air arsenal.

The look of the North American Aviation O-47 was typical 1930s. First flown in 1935, some 238 examples of the observation plane were built by NAA in Inglewood, California. This example was photographed over Yosemite in 1938. By the time America went to war, the O-47 was an outmoded design. Soon after, the old aircraft was relegated to patrol and utility duties. (NA/USAAF.)

A North American BT-9 training plane cruises over the circular center of Randolph Field, nicknamed the "West Point of the Air." Some 260 BT-9s were built for the military at a price of $20,000 each. Many flyers claimed the planes had unsettling stall and spin characteristics, which led to improved versions of the aircraft. One upgraded version of the plane with retractable landing gear paved the way for North American's famous AT-6 Texan. (NA/USAAF.)

While many Southern California aircraft companies struggled in the prewar years of the 1930s, North American was comparatively rich. Large contracts with the US Army, US Navy, and foreign governments building training airplanes kept the company in the black. This is the Inglewood factory in July 1938. (NA/USAAF.)

Most of the famous Allied flyers of World War II completed their training in a plane like this before heading into combat in fighters and bombers. North American's versatile and dependable two-seat trainer was designated the AT-6 Texan by the Army Air Corps, the SNJ by the Navy, and the Harvard in Great Britain and Canada. Nearly 15,500 of the planes were built. (NA/USAAF.)

Versions of the AT-6 Texan were used to teach flyers how to operate relatively powerful and complex aircraft before moving on to an all-out warplane. Primary training came first, then basic training. After that, students moved up to several weeks of advanced training. Here, cadets get a lecture before beginning the final phase of training and earning their wings. (NA/USAAF.)

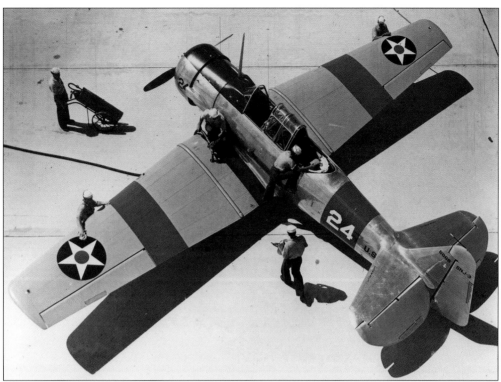

The Texan/SNJ was usually heavier and faster than anything a flying cadet had operated before. The plane was powered by a nine-cylinder Pratt & Whitney R-1340 Wasp engine that generated roughly 600 horsepower. The plane's two seats were arranged in tandem, each with a set of flight controls. Commonly, the student flew in front and the instructor in the back. (NA/USN.)

It was easy to make mistakes when learning to fly, such as being a little too heavy on the brakes while coming in for a landing. This Texan somersaulted at a training airfield near St. Joseph, Missouri, on April 18, 1945. The plane's tail came up suddenly, burying the trainer's nose in the dirt and initiating an embarrassing and painful experience for this student pilot. (NA/USAAF.)

US aviation schools did not teach only Americans to fly during World War II. Students from allies all over the world came to learn their trade on Texan and SNJ training planes—Canada, Mexico, Great Britain, China, and South America. In some extreme cases, the students were not only learning to fly, they were simultaneously receiving a crash course in the English language at the same time! Here, flyers from Latin America earn their wings at a Navy training base in Corpus Christi, Texas, in 1942. (NA/USN.)

A photograph of the flight line at Naval Air Station Corpus Christi, the "University of the Air," shows dozens of SNJs ready for the day's lessons in November 1942. The military's big training bases tended to be in the American South, where the terrain was expansive and flat and the weather was good for year-round flying. (NA/USN.)

The commander of World War II's "Tuskegee Airmen," the United States' first African American combat flyers, learned his trade in a North American AT-6 Texan. Benjamin O. Davis is seen here climbing into his Texan trainer plane at Tuskegee Army Airfield in Alabama in January 1942. He was the first black officer to solo in an Army aircraft, and he was one of the first five African American graduates of the program. He went on to fly 60 combat missions in Europe as the leader of the 332nd Fighter Group. (NA/USAAF.)

A Navy SNJ-4 wheels in the clear skies over Florida in 1942. Even with a full schedule of rigorous training, there was always a little time to have some fun. Aerobatics, after all, were a way to learn. Flyers who became familiar with the limits of their aircraft could fearlessly push them right to the edge in combat and occasionally beyond. (NA/USN.)

A flight school was the home for thousands of nonflying support staff. For each student or instructor, there were a dozen or more soldiers and sailors who were cooks, builders, machinists, laborers, physicians, and so on. Here, a pair of Navy mechanics work on the propeller of an SNJ-4 at Naval Air Station Corpus Christi in November 1942. (NA/USN.)

North American's AT-6/SNJ design had staying power. In this photograph, taken in 1950, a jet-powered Lockheed P-80 Shooting Star fighter streaks past this Texan like it is standing still. But the Texan was far from useless, even in the Jet Age. The planes went into combat with American forces for the first time during the Korean War and were used as forward air controllers. Flying "low and slow," Texans were used to scout targets for the fast-moving jets. (NA/USAAF.)

Normal takeoff speed for an SNJ was 80 miles per hour. If wind gusts reached that speed, the plane could leap into the air from a standstill and tumble away. As a hurricane approaches a training base in Florida, maintenance crews have carefully put the planes on their bellies, firmly tethered them to the tarmac, and affixed hearty gust locks to the control surfaces to save them from destruction. This photograph was most likely taken at Saufley Field, near Pensacola, in the mid-1950s. (NMoNA.)

North American Aviation had never designed a fighter before it built the plane that would become the P-51 Mustang, arguably the best fighter of World War II. This is the NA-73X Mustang prototype in flight over California. The plane was involved in a crash at Miles Field (today the location of Los Angeles International Airport), but designers knew almost from the beginning that they had a real winner on their hands. (SMMoF.)

The Mustang was originally designed for the British. Here, workers carefully crate a Mustang Mk 1 at the NAA Inglewood plant for overseas shipment to a Royal Air Force tactical unit. Not all of them made it. German U-boats sunk cargo ships carrying 25 or more "fresh from the factory" Mustangs during attacks in the North Atlantic. (SMMoF.)

North American's famous Mustang fighter began service with the US Army with the thankless job of lugging bombs to the front lines. The attack version of the Mustang was designated the A-36 Apache and was used in North Africa early in the war. The plane was an excellent and stable dive bomber. The plane's dive flaps, a design borrowed from Vultee, can be seen on the top and bottom of this Apache's right wing. (SMMoF.)

Six ground crewmen lift a 500-pound bomb into position on the wing pylon of *Robbie*, an A-36A Apache based in the Mediterranean. Later that day, the weapons would find their way to a German or Italian stronghold as Allied forces pushed northward. Apaches stayed in service until the early part of 1944. By that time, about half the 500 A-36s built had been destroyed in accidents or in combat. (NA/USAAF.)

Upon arrival in Great Britain, a new P-51A Mustang gets a bath. The plane was covered with oily preservative to keep from corroding in the salt air during its voyage across the Atlantic aboard an English cargo ship. The A-model Mustangs were powered by an Allison V-1710 engine, which kept the plane from reaching its full potential in the early days. (NA/USAAF.)

Loaded with a pair of 75-gallon external fuel tanks, *Mrs. Virginia* of the 1st Air Commando Group cruises over Chin Hills in China. This P-51A has had a hard life, as seen by the exhaust stains, mud, and dust covering its skin. Most airfields in the Far East were carved from the jungle with runways made from crushed rock. While a majority of the planes assigned to Europe came straight from the factories, flyers in the Pacific made do with whatever they could get. This photograph was taken in the summer of 1944. (NA/USAAF.)

It was not enough to build thousands of aircraft. Each California plane company had to prove that every machine was ready for combat. Corps of test flyers, like these men working for North American Aviation, spent their days taking each airplane up, "wringing it out," and bringing it home for military acceptance. The young test pilot on the right is George Welch, a former Army pilot who claimed four enemy aircraft during the Japanese attack on Pearl Harbor. After he retired from the military he went to work for NAA testing Mustangs. Sadly, he was killed in the crash of a North American F-100 Super Sabre jet fighter in 1954 near Edwards Air Force Base. (SMMoF.)

Flyers said that the cockpit layout of the P-51 Mustang was excellent. This is partly because most of them had previously flown North American's AT-6 in training, which had a similar arrangement. Basic flight instruments stood in the boxed-in area to the left, engine and prop controls were on the left side, and communications and electrical were on the right. Between the pilot's knees were the weaponry controls. The odd-shaped dial near the stick was the fuel tank selector. (SMMoF.)

Red-tailed *Stinky* of the Tuskegee Airmen is captured in this image between combat missions in Italy. In the foreground, an armorer feeds belts of .50-caliber ammunition into the wing of another P-51B Mustang. At the time, Army units were still deeply segregated. The entire 332nd Fighter Group was made up of black pilots and ground crews. (NA/USAAF.)

Pictured here are two innovations that helped the Mustang become one of the best fighter aircraft of World War II. First, P-51B Mustangs and beyond had a Packard-built copy of a supercharged Rolls-Royce engine. The new power helped the plane operate at great heights. Second was the external fuel tank, which allowed the Mustang to stick with the bombers over long distances, protecting them from marauding Luftwaffe fighters. (NA/USAAF.)

Over the Alps, bubble-canopied P-51Ds cruise in formation. These planes are flown by the group commanders of the four fighter P-51 Mustang units of the 15th Air Force: the 325th Fighter Group, also known as Checkertail Clan, in the foreground; the 322nd Fighter Group, also known as the Tuskegee Airmen; the 52nd Fighter Group, and the 31st Fighter Group. (NA/USAAF.)

Sky Bouncer of the 375th Fighter Squadron is seen on a bomber escort mission over Europe. One of the Mustang's most distinctive characteristics was the plane's belly scoop, which contained oil coolers and a radiator. The location of the scoop was chosen to keep the fighter as aerodynamically clean as possible. *Sky Bouncer* was wrecked in a takeoff accident in April 1945. (NA/USAAF.)

This group of Mustangs of the 375th Fighter Group illustrates North American's adjustments to the Mustang's design in wartime. The plane farthest from the camera is the oldest, a California-built P-51B with a "razorback" cockpit. Next is a bubble-canopied P-51D, also built at NAA's Inglewood factory. When the reduction of the plane's fuselage led to instability, designers added a small dorsal fin in front of the horizontal tail of P-51Ds. The modification can be seen on the aircraft closest to the camera. (NA/USAAF.)

In front of the weather-beaten P-51D *Lady Gwen II*, flyers Glenn Stapp (left) and William Manahan of the 350th Fighter Squadron discuss an engagement over Europe. Typical of pilots, Manahan uses his hands to explain the particulars of their dogfight. The Mustang has an extra rearview mirror mounted on top of its cockpit—most likely stolen from a downed Spitfire fighter. (NA/USAAF.)

At a California port, a new Mustang, sans propeller, tail planes, and wing tips, is loaded into the hull of a cargo ship in April 1944. The Platiphane-covered plane would arrive in an Asian port a few weeks later, ready to join the US Army Air Forces in combatting the Japanese armies in China. Note the Army representatives, only semi-interested in the loading process, standing at lower left. (NA/OoWI.)

A P-51 Mustang receives "invasion stripes" on the afternoon before the D-Day attacks on Axis armies in France. Today, warbird restorers apply the lines to their antique aircraft exactly 18 inches apart, with painstaking skill and uniformity. During the war, crew chiefs slopped the paint out on their entire squadron of battered and bleached aircraft in just a few hours—freehand—usually with house paint. (NA/USAAF.)

In the last stages of the war in Europe, a P-51 Mustang of the 356th Fighter Squadron is readied for service at a former German airfield near Frankfurt, Germany. The remains of a blasted and burned Focke-Wulf Fw 190 fighter lie in the foreground. This photograph was taken in the spring of 1945. (NA/USAAF.)

In some of the longest fighter missions of the war, Mustangs based on the island of Iwo Jima flew eight-plus hour missions over the Pacific to attack Japan's home islands. VLR (Very Long Range) missions tested the resiliency of both the planes and their pilots. This piece of nose art, cynically stealing a homefront tire conservation slogan, seemed humorously appropriate to the flyers who cruised over hundreds of miles of dangerous seas to wage brief attacks on enemy airfields and ports before turning for home. (NA/USAAF.)

Mustangs soldiered on after World War II, serving in Korea as attack planes. Redesignated F-51s, the venerable vets lobbed bombs and rockets at the front lines while sophisticated jet fighters took over the job of hunting enemy aircraft in the skies above. This photograph shows Dallas-built F-51D Ol' NaDSoB, the last D-model Mustang made by North American Aviation. Serving with the 18th Fighter Bomber Group, the plane was lost in Korea in October 1951. (NA/USAF.)

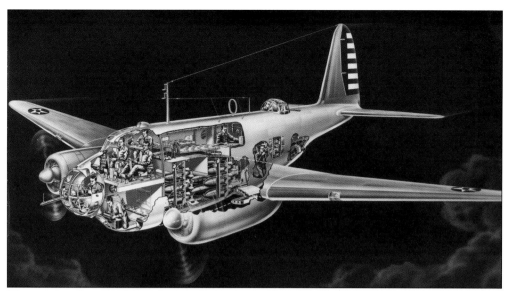

This concept drawing shows the North American XB-21 bomber. The plane was evaluated along with the Douglas B-18 in 1937. By all accounts, the North American plane was a better aircraft, but the Douglas bomber was cheaper. A B-18 cost $64,000, while the price tag for a B-21 would have been around $121,000. Only one XB-21 aircraft was ever built. (SMMoF.)

The North American NA-40B was pitted against similar aircraft in the Army's evaluations in 1939. In the end, they again ordered a Douglas design—the A-20 Havoc. However, an improved version of NAA's bomber, redesignated the NA-62, was back for more testing six months later. That aircraft became one of the company's most successful World War II aircraft, the B-25 Mitchell. (NA/USAAF.)

At a wind tunnel in Inglewood, a North American model maker fusses over a large-scale mahogany model of the B-25. The replica bomber is equipped with an experimental lower turret, and the worker holds an exact replica of the plane's payload, a torpedo. Though hardly ever used, the B-25 could be equipped with an external rack to hold a Mark 13 torpedo. (NA/USAAF.)

Proud papas come to California to pick up their new plane, the first B-25 Mitchell to be delivered to the Army. The new plane would be assigned to the 17th Bombardment Group based at McChord Field near Tacoma, Washington. Here, the flyers pose briefly for a photograph before their trip north. The first of over 9,800 Mitchells joined the Army in February 1941. On December 24 of that same year, one of the unit's B-25s dropped bombs on a Japanese submarine spotted at the mouth of the Columbia River. (SMMoF.)

The B-25 Mitchell is perhaps most famous for its participation in the Doolittle Raid. On April 18, 1942, a group of 16 big B-25s took off from the diminutive deck of the USS *Hornet* and bombed targets in Japan. The bombing had little military value, but the morale boost for the United States was significant at that early stage in the war. Here, one of the bombers prepares to take off. Note the lines on the deck to keep the big plane in the right place. (NA/USAAF.)

When Franklin Roosevelt was questioned by the press as to where Doolittle's B-25 bombers had come from, he wryly told them, "Shangri-La." Months later, when Lt. Col. Jimmy Doolittle visited NAA's plant in Inglewood, he told the assembled workers, "Don't tell a soul, but Shangri-La is right here at this North American plant. Our bombers—your bombers—functioned magnificently." (NA/USAAF.)

In Italy, the biggest one-day killer of B-25s was not enemy flak or fighters, it was nature. In the middle of a war zone, Mount Vesuvius rumbled to life and flash-fried more than 80 combat-ready Mitchells parked at Poggiomarino (Pompeii's airport). This photograph shows a 310th Bomb Squadron aircraft after being doused with super-heated ash on the night of March 22, 1944. (NA/USAAF.)

In the Pacific and China, the role of the B-25 Mitchell changed over time. Once a medium-altitude bomber, more and more missions involved brutalizing Japanese airfields, ships, and bridges at low level. Ever-ingenious aircrew hot-rodded their planes to complete the task. This Mitchell of the 490th Bomb Group (the "Burma Bridge Busters") has six .50-caliber guns stuffed into its nose where the bombardier usually flies. (NA/USAAF.)

North American responded to the need for "gunship" versions of the Mitchell. This plane, a B-25H, is readied for service at NAA in Inglewood. The plane has 10 machine guns, and that big portside recess holds something even more punishing—a gun the size of the main cannon of a Sherman tank! Some pilots said that the recoil from firing the airframe-mounted 75-mm cannon was so powerful it would slow the big bomber's airspeed by a few knots. The weapon was ideal for taking on ships. (SMMoF.)

A Mitchell of the 499th Bomb Squadron (the "Bats Outta Hell") makes a low pass over a Japanese destroyer escort in Taiwan Strait in April 1945. The B-25J's nose has been upgraded with a package of eight .50-caliber guns and a striking wraparound painting of a wicked-looking bat that covers much of the front of the fuselage. This photograph was taken from the tail gun position of another B-25 making its run just forward of the plane pictured. (NA/USAAF.)

Bones of the 82nd Bomb Squadron was the last B-25 to be built at the Inglewood factory. As the plane went into final assembly, North American workers began to tape dollar bills on the plane and sign their names on its Alclad skin. The money went to the Army-Navy relief fund, but the names stayed put as the plane arrived in India in November 1944. The press quoted the pilot as saying, "*Bones* is a running fool. We love this ship." (NA/USAAF.)

Joseph Heller's classic novel *Catch-22* involved a B-25 flyer who could no longer sweat and pray his way through dangerous missions. This plane, a NAA Kansas City–built B-25J, made it through 127 straight combat missions without an abort. Here, crew chief T.Sgt. Alexander Reams proudly poses with his steed. However, *Sweat and Pray*'s luck eventually ran out. On April 20, 1945, the plane was lost in a nonfatal crash landing near Rimini, Italy. (NA/USAAF.)

How does one cover hundreds of thousands of square feet of sprawling factory floor? Get a bike. Here, a female clerk catches up with a foreman on her skip-tooth cruiser on the ramp outside the Inglewood factory. The War Department asked California workers to ride to and from their jobs as well. If the employee lived just a few miles away from the factory, they were strongly encouraged to commute by bicycle to save fuel, rubber, and oil. (NA/OoWI.)

Marine flyers examine a 65-foot-long scroll signed by 35,000 Oklahoma City schoolchildren. Each student donated 10¢ to the purchase of their PBJ bomber (the naval designation for the B-25). They asked that the aviators drop the scroll over enemy territory. The Marine flyers deposited the scroll, along with a load of bombs, on a Japanese airfield near Rabaul in the summer of 1944. (NA/USMC.)

The North American XB-28 bomber was a great airplane, but NAA's Inglewood facility was overrun with more important wartime projects at the time of its first flight in 1942. A version modified for high-altitude reconnaissance never made it to the Army. During a test flight, North American Aviation pilots were forced to bail out of the plane during an uncontrollable dive off the coast. This photograph is said to depict the plane moments before its final flight on August 4, 1943. The caption reads, "Lost it over Newport Beach; Pilots wet, but O.K." (SMMoF.)

P-51 Mustangs were involved in some of the longest fighter missions of the war. The idea of a long-range, two-pilot version of the plane that could span great distances over the Pacific came about in late 1943. While the XP-82 looked simply like two Mustangs spliced together, nearly everything on the new fighter had to be designed from scratch. The first plane flew in June 1945. This aircraft, the second XP-82 Twin Mustang, was photographed near Muroc Field (today Edwards Air Force Base) that same year. (NA/USAAF.)

Five

VULTEE, HUGHES, NORTHROP, AND RYAN

Some of Southern California's small plane companies were consumed by aircraft-making behemoths during World War II. Vultee (and Michigan-based Stinson) merged with San Diego's Consolidated Aircraft Corporation in 1943. Vega, a subsidiary of Lockheed Aircraft Corporation, was fully integrated by that same year.

Other organizations stayed fiercely independent. Hughes Aircraft Company, headed by aviator and film producer Howard Hughes, worked with the Army to create radical aircraft like the massive wooden HK-1 (H-4) "Spruce Goose" and the XF-11 high-speed reconnaissance plane. Both aircraft fell behind schedule and did not make their first flights until after the end of the war.

Hughes Aircraft, however, had an impact on Los Angeles wartime production making aircraft components. A large corps of Hughes employees built parts for nearly every warplane of the era. Plastic-impregnated, heat-molded plywood—called Duramold—was used for aircraft wing panels when metal was scarce. Hughes-built ammunition booster motors and flexible feed chutes reliably pulled belts of .50-caliber ammunition into waiting guns to alleviate jamming.

Northrop Aircraft Inc. of Hawthorne, California, primarily built the P-61 Black Widow during the war. The twin-engine, twin-boom aircraft was America's first purpose-built night fighter. A radar system in the plane's fiberglass nose helped the plane track down enemy aircraft at night or in bad weather. The Black Widow finished the job with four machine guns and four 20-mm cannon.

Northrop had 9,200 employees at the height of production. The company made 1,107 planes during the war (January 1940 to August 1945), including 706 Black Widows. This number represents just 0.3 percent of America's output.

San Diego–based Ryan Aeronautical Company built 1,485 military aircraft between January 1940 to August 1945. Over 1,200 of these aircraft were primary training planes, used to teach young military cadets how to fly. Near the end of the war, Ryan developed a peculiar dual-powered Navy fighter, equipped with both a conventional radial engine and a jet. Less than 70 Ryan Fireballs were built before the end of 1945.

Ryan employed 8,600 San Diego men and women at the height of production during wartime. Their products represent 0.5 percent of America's total World War II aircraft arsenal.

Before Consolidated and Vultee merged, the latter built thousands of military aircraft at its factory in Downey, California. In this image, a line of Vultee Vengeance dive bombers are readied for the Royal Air Force in June 1942. Flyers said that the planes were vulnerable and could not survive in most combat environments. As a result, many were sent to the Far East. Others became utility planes far from the front lines. (NA/USAAF.)

The strange case of the TBY Sea Wolf starts with the fact that it was a torpedo bomber designed by the Chance Vought Corporation. During wartime, Vought was so overloaded with demand for Corsair fighters that the government chose Vultee to complete an order for 1,100 planes. By the time Vultee converted a former truck-making factory in Allentown, Pennsylvania, the company had merged with Consolidated. Only 180 were made before the end of World War II. None of the aircraft saw combat. (NMoNA.)

The BT-13 Valiant was the most produced Vultee aircraft. Over 9,500 were built in Downey, California, before and during World War II. In this type of aircraft, cadets learned to fly in formation, operate at night, and travel long distances. While the BT-13 was officially named the Valiant, nearly every flyer called it the "Vultee Vibrator." This one was assigned to Minter Field near Shafter, California. (Author's collection.)

At the Downey factory, women workers assemble the welded steel tube fuselages of BT-13s. Unlike modern aircraft, where the skin takes part of the structural load, the Vultee trainer had a burly inner structure with skin affixed to the outside. At this point in the assembly process, the fuselages move through on an overhead conveyor system, and the workers of Department 90 are stationed in one fixed location on the Vultee factory floor. (NA/OoWI.)

An Office of War Information photographer captured this moment in the construction process when a new Pratt & Whitney R-985 Wasp Junior engine is bolted to the firewall of the plane. Note the overhead crane system holding two more engines for the next aircraft in line. At the time, the Vultee factory was in the midst of building a block of SNVs, the Navy version of the BT-13. (NA/OoWI.)

With their rolling toolbox, a four-woman "speed installation" crew works on a BT-13 that has recently left the factory. It was important to not hold up the line of aircraft constantly moving toward completion. Sometimes things got missed or intentionally skipped in order to keep Uncle Sam's armada of new aircraft efficiently flowing. Teams like this cruised Vultee's ramp to clean up the slack, screw on the last components, and get each aircraft ready for its first test flight. (NA/OoWI.)

Posing for a public relations shot, women hold up power tools used to pre-assemble the components surrounding a trainer's R-985 engine. Sticking to the adage, "Don't let them get too big, too fast," the nose of the plane, firewall forward, was nearly completed when it was finally joined to the fuselage (seen on the previous page). This photograph was taken in 1943 in Downey, California. (NA/OoWI.)

Skillfully working a rivet machine, a young lady assembles fairing parts for Valiant aircraft in this promotional photograph. Her short pin curl hairstyle (with a ribbon) is fashionable and efficient—still perfectly acceptable to the factory's shop foreman. Many women working for aircraft companies had brothers, husbands, or boyfriends who were serving overseas. While soldiers and sailors fought in the Pacific or in Europe, women looked to hasten the end of the conflict by taking a tough, dirty, and demanding factory job. (NA/OoWI.)

As the tails of SNV trainers are assembled at Downey, an Office of War Information employee captured this photograph of a small man working at the Vultee factory. While shunned from military service, aircraft plants actively searched out little people to build airplanes. As one source explains, "The assembly line also employed 'midgets' who were recruited from circus sideshows and the entertainment industry. They proved invaluable for confined space assembly tasks, such as crawling inside wingtips to buck rivets." (NA/OoWI.)

While the Vultee plant boasted "more automatic machinery per square foot than any other aircraft factory," sometimes it simply came down to construction methods that have been around for decades, and manpower—or more accurately, womanpower. Here, smoke curls from the top of an exhaust stack as a worker welds its seams. Her job is to finish the tacked-together piece with a nice, even union along every inch of the two halves. (NA/OoWI.)

"Make something weird, but also wonderful," the Army's 1940 R-40C seemed to say. The military wanted to push the boundaries with aircraft design more radical than the standard monoplane fighter. Vultee submitted a strange looking aircraft that would become the XP-54. The workers in the Vultee plant dubbed it the "Swoose Goose." The plane won the design competition but was hampered by ever-growing weight concerns and an unproven engine. Only two were built. (NA/USAAF.)

When Germany rolled through much of Europe behind waves of Stuka dive bombers, the world took notice. Vultee got the task of creating powerful, maneuverable bombers for the Army. By the time the plane flew for the first time in early 1944, the Army had changed its mind about the role and value of the XA-41. Existing fighters like the P-47 Thunderbolt and P-51 Mustang were being successfully employed as fighter bombers, and the need for a specialized attack plane faded. Only one XA-41 was built. (NA/USAAF.)

Blending the performance of a jet with the dependability of the turboprop engine, the Consolidated Vultee XP-81 could zoom circles around nearly any enemy aircraft. Interestingly, it was the underpowered turboprop engine that gave the designers and Army more trouble than the turbojet. The plane flew for the first time in February 1945; as the war progressed, it seemed the new fighter would not be needed. Two were built before the project was cancelled. (NA/USAAF.)

Howard Hughes poses with his sleek H-1 racer in 1935. It was the first Hughes Aircraft Company design. In September 1935, Hughes flew (and crashed) the speedy plane for the first time. Many World War II–era aviation historians and Hughes himself claimed (inaccurately) that Mitsubishi stole many of the H-1's design traits when it created the A6M Zero Japanese naval fighter. (SMMoF.)

Hughes Aircraft did not complete any aircraft during World War II, but Hughes parts and components went into nearly every Southern California warplane. Gun motors and feed chutes built by the company efficiently and quickly coaxed belts of .50-caliber bullets in guns like these, seen in the waist area of a Consolidated B-24 bomber. (NA/USAAF.)

Hughes's fast, long-range reconnaissance plane was ordered by the Army in September 1943, though some suspected he would never deliver. Orders for 100 of the planes were cancelled in May 1945, and it was July 7, 1946, before the first XF-11 took to the skies. During the initial test flight, one of the plane's complex contra-rotating propellers malfunctioned, and Hughes crashed the aircraft into a neighborhood in Beverly Hills. Hughes was severely injured in the crash. (SMMoF.)

The H-4 (HK-1) "Spruce Goose" aircraft originated as a way to transport large batches of cargo and men across the U-boat–infested Atlantic. In order to conserve critical war materials, much of the plane was built from wood. Delays plagued the project, and Hughes's partner Henry Kaiser backed out. The plane did not fly until November 1947, more than two years after the end of World War II. (SMMoF.)

Northrop's wicked looking glossy black P-61 Black Widow night fighter cruises over the Los Angeles coastline near the Palos Verdes Peninsula. The twin-engine, twin-boomed plane carried a crew of three and a collection of cannon and machine guns. It was the first American combat plane to be purpose-built as a night fighter and the first designed with an airborne radar system. (SMMoF.)

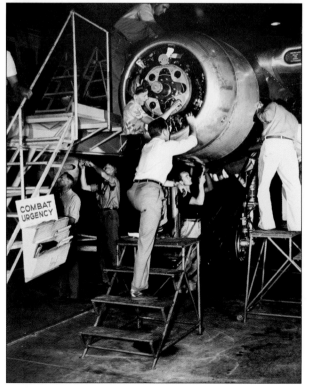

Northrop built over 700 P-61s at its factory in Hawthorne, California. Aft sections of the P-61B aircraft appear in the foreground, joined with noses on the right side of the aisle. Beyond, entire fuselages are lifted high to include the nose wheel. On the left, nearly completed planes are visible after they have "turned the corner," headed toward the paint shop. (SMMoF.)

The Army considered the night fighters vital for combat operations. Unlike Douglas, Consolidated, or North American, Northrop was a comparatively small company. When word came down that they needed to step up their production, Northrop employees raised their construction numbers by an amazing 30 percent. (NA/USAAF.)

Early versions of the Black Widow flew with milky white Plexiglas noses covering their SCR-720 radar. Here, a backlit P-61A is seen off the California coastline. Later versions of the plane had tougher fiberglass noses that were routinely painted black. The radar could detect a fighter-sized flying object at five miles and large bombers at 10 miles. (NA/USAAF.)

The crew of a 9th Air Force Black Widow stands by their plane, awaiting sunset. The planes worked to patrol the night skies near the front, protecting Allied forward bases from enemy bombers sneaking in under cover of darkness. Often, the plane's three-man crew was reduced to two, omitting the gunner, who rode in the seat behind the pilot. The pair remaining was the radar operator (left) and the pilot (right). (NA/USAAF.)

At a base on the Mariana Islands, crewmen load the four 20-mm cannons in the belly of a 6th Night Fighter Squadron P-61. The heavy cannon were meant to knock out anything the Black Widow encountered in the night skies with a swift blow. One flight crew whose dog flew with them on missions related that Rags was not fazed by much of anything. But when the 20-mm cannons grumbled to life, Rags did his best to find a place to hide. (NA/USAAF.)

With the plane's two Double Wasp engines thundering, the pilot of a P-61A in the Pacific prepares to take off amid a cloud of oily smoke. *Midnight Mickey* served with the 6th Night Fighter Squadron on Saipan. This photograph was taken in July 1944. Just days after the war ended, *Mickey* was reclaimed as salvage. (NA/USAAF.)

This photograph shows the "front office" of a Northrop Black Widow. The image was captured in Culver City, California, as an Army motion picture unit prepared to film *How to Fly the P-61*. The plane's control yoke, cranked all the way to the left, has two trigger buttons—one for the machine guns and one for the cannons. (NA/USAAF.)

The Spook, of the 548th Night Fighter Squadron, returned to Iwo Jima at night in a fog bank. While attempting to make a landing with the assistance of an approach radar, a crosswind pushed the Black Widow off to one side of the runway where it struck another P-61. When the sun came up, a photographer captured the aftermath. (NA/USAAF.)

A severely weather-beaten P-61C cruises over the American Midwest in the years after World War II. Some 41 of the upgraded Black Widows were built before the Army shut the line down. The C-model aircraft were speedy, powerful, and able to carry additional fuel. The plane also had speed brakes, allowing it to race up to its prey and then slow down when in gun range. (NA/USAAF.)

One of the competitors to Vultee's XP-54 was Northrop's submission, the tailless XP-56 Black Bullet. Similar to the XP-54, the XP-56 had a pusher engine and a radical airframe design that proved to be more complex than standard pursuit planes. The first of two prototypes (pictured) flew in September 1943. It was subsequently wrecked during a high-speed taxi test at Muroc Dry Lake later that year. (NA/USAAF.)

During World War II, San Diego–based Ryan Aeronautical Company made hundreds of military trainers. The first was a derivative of the Ryan ST (Sport Trainer), initially flown in 1934. The aircraft pictured is a militarized version of the plane, designated YPT-16, seen during evaluation around 1939. (NA/USAAF.)

The next step in the evolution of Ryan's ST was the PT-20A, fitted with a 125-horsepower Kinner engine. Kinner Motors Inc. was founded in Glendale, California. Here, one third of the entire fleet that was built is on display in San Diego before delivery to the Army. (NA/USAAF.)

Ryan's most produced primary trainer was the PT-22 Recruit. Production topped out for this version of the venerable ST at 1,048 aircraft. Here, a squadron of the handsome-looking aircraft are parked in a "V for Victory" formation outside Ryan's factory in San Diego. Student pilots most often agree that the plane was a little bit of a challenge to a young flyer just starting out. (NA/USAAF.)

The Navy bought versions of the Ryan ST as well. The NR-1 was equivalent to the Army's PT-21. In this image, a pair of NR-1s buzz over Florida's flat topography during a wartime training session. The Navy purchased 100 of the planes. Note that these are students out on their own, sitting in the front seat. Many flyers related that the trainer did not behave very well when flown from the back with the front seat unoccupied. (NMoNA.)

US Navy WAVES (Women Accepted for Volunteer Emergency Service) go to work on a pair of Ryan NR-1 trainers at a repair depot in Florida. For most of the war, WAVES were restricted to duties within the United States, allowing more sailors to fight overseas. By the end of the war, about 2.5 percent of the Navy's total strength was women. (NA/USN.)

Pilots testing the Ryan FR-1 Fireball prototype would flummox Navy pilots they encountered over San Diego by effortlessly zooming by with their propeller at a standstill. The Fireball had two sources of power, a dependable R-1820 radial engine up front and a General Electric turbojet installed aft of the pilot. The Navy ordered more than 1,000 of what would be its first jet-powered aircraft; however, only 71 were built before the end of the war and the shutdown of Ryan's assembly line. (NA/USN.)

A Ryan Fireball takes off from San Diego Airport in 1945. The unique plane carried a jet engine for performance and a piston-powered radial for dependable, immediate power for dangerous landings aboard aircraft carriers. Some wry pilots observed that the plane's name, Fireball, was actually the situation they were most trying to avoid when flying the strange little aircraft. Note Consolidated Vultee's collection of new tall-tailed B-32 bombers in the background. (NA/USN.)

With the Consolidated factory as its backdrop, Ryan's YO-51 Dragonfly leaps into the skies over San Diego. The observation aircraft had excellent short takeoff and landing characteristics and could fly at speeds down to 30 miles per hour. The Army, however, chose a Stinson design. Months later, Stinson was acquired by California's Vultee Aircraft Corporation. (NA/USAAF.)

DISCOVER THOUSANDS OF LOCAL HISTORY BOOKS FEATURING MILLIONS OF VINTAGE IMAGES

Arcadia Publishing, the leading local history publisher in the United States, is committed to making history accessible and meaningful through publishing books that celebrate and preserve the heritage of America's people and places.

Find more books like this at
www.arcadiapublishing.com

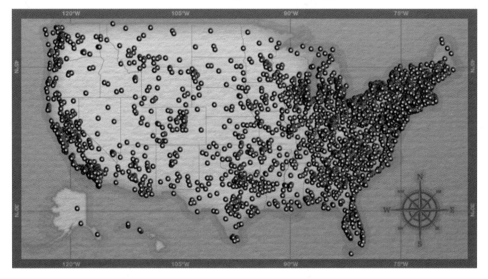

Search for your hometown history, your old stomping grounds, and even your favorite sports team.